# THE JOURNAL OF A
# TOUR TO CORSICA

JAMES BOSWELL

(In the dress of an armed Corsican Chief)

# The *Journal* of a Tour to CORSICA; & Memoirs of PASCAL PAOLI
## By JAMES BOSWELL, Esq.

*Olim meminisse juvabit.*
VIRG.

Edited, with an introduction,
by S. C. ROBERTS

*CAMBRIDGE*
AT THE UNIVERSITY PRESS
1929

CAMBRIDGE
UNIVERSITY PRESS

University Printing House, Cambridge CB2 8BS, United Kingdom

Cambridge University Press is part of the University of Cambridge.

It furthers the University's mission by disseminating knowledge in the pursuit of
education, learning and research at the highest international levels of excellence.

www.cambridge.org
Information on this title: www.cambridge.org/9781107502192

First edition 1923
First published 1923
Reprinted 1929
First paperback edition 2015

*A catalogue record for this publication is available from the British Library*

ISBN 978-1-107-50219-2 Paperback

# CONTENTS

# NOTE

ON THE

SECOND IMPRESSION

In this impression I have taken the opportunity of correcting a chronological error on p. viii and of recording a small bibliographical discovery on p. xvii.

S.C.R.

*January* 1929

# INTRODUCTION

AT a time when James Boswell is coming into his own, it seems fitting that the work which won him his earliest literary fame should once more be made available.

*The Journal of a Tour to Corsica* was first published, together with *An Account of Corsica*, in February, 1768. A second edition appeared in the June of the same year and a third, with corrections and a congratulatory letter from Lord Lyttelton, in 1769. Since that date, the *Tour* has been reprinted but once and then only in company with, and somewhat under the shadow of, the *Letters between Erskine and Boswell* which Dr Birkbeck Hill edited in 1879.

Such is the bibliographical justification for the present edition, in which the *Tour* appears by itself for the first time. For thus tearing it out of its original context there is, of course, the highest authority:

"Your History," wrote Johnson to Boswell on 9 September 1769, "is like other histories, but your Journal is in a very high degree curious and delightful. There is between the History and the Journal that difference which there will always be found between notions borrowed from without, and notions generated within. Your History was copied from books; your Journal rose out of your own experience and observation. You express images which operated strongly upon yourself, and you have impressed them with great force upon your readers. I know not whether I could name any narrative by which curiosity is better excited, or better gratified."[1]

The first point to be remembered about the early career of James Boswell is that, as Birkbeck Hill remarks, he was 'Corsica' Boswell long before he was 'Johnson' Boswell.

The famous meeting in Tom Davies's back parlour took place in May 1763. In the August of the same year Boswell left for Utrecht. During the intervening months the friendship had quickly ripened; Boswell had visited Johnson in his chambers and had entertained him at the Mitre. When Boswell left for Harwich, Johnson insisted on accompanying him. "I hope, Sir," said Boswell when they parted, "you will not forget me in my absence." "Nay Sir," replied Johnson, "it is more likely you should forget me, than that I should forget you."

Still, though Johnson had thus early surrendered to Boswell's good humour, the friendship was only just begun; Boswell had only just achieved the supreme intimacy of accompanying Johnson on his late, tea-drinking visits to Mrs Anna Williams.

The primary object of Boswell's foreign travel was a course of legal study at Utrecht; but he was of the age when the eighteenth-century gentleman

---

[1] It is, however, worth remark that the *Account of Corsica* has recently found a defender in Mr Leonard Whibley (*Blackwood's Magazine*, March, 1923).

properly made the grand tour—and much of Boswell's life was a grand tour in quest of famous men.

Growing tired of the law schools of Utrecht, he passed from Holland into Germany. From Berlin he wrote: "I may either steer to Italy or to France. I shall see Voltaire. I shall also see Switzerland and Rousseau; these two men are to me greater objects than most statues or pictures."

All these aims were duly accomplished. In Italy Boswell contrived to meet John Wilkes, then in exile, and together they made the ascent of Vesuvius; at Ferney he visited Voltaire with whom he discussed the subject of natural religion; and at Motiers he presented himself before Rousseau. In Professor Tinker's recent book we are enabled to read for the first time Boswell's remarkable letter of self-introduction:

Open your door, then, Sir, to a man who dares to say that he deserves to enter there. Trust a unique foreigner. You will never repent it[1].

It was Rousseau who gave Boswell an introduction to Pasquale Paoli, the Corsican hero, and it was Paoli who inspired Boswell's first literary achievement.

It is not easy to appreciate fully at the present

[1] See *Young Boswell*, pp. 49–58. After Boswell had left, Rousseau wrote to him at Geneva, enclosing a letter to Deleyre at Parma. The enclosure was not sealed and Boswell characteristically thanked Rousseau for this mark of confidence. "Il se trompe," wrote Rousseau, "ce n'est qu'une marque d'étourderie" (Rousseau to Deleyre, 11 Feb. 1765).

day the appeal of Corsica to Boswell's romantic sensibility. There were several elements in this appeal: first, there was Boswell's characteristic desire for novelty, for something that would make him personally conspicuous—"I wished for something more than just the common course of what is called the tour of Europe; and Corsica occurred to me as a place which no body else had seen"; secondly, there was the attraction of a heroic figure to be interviewed and Boswellised; and lastly, there was the peculiar appeal of Corsica itself. Throughout his tour Boswell was agreeably conscious of the feeling of a return to a simpler way of life, to that 'state of nature' which was the theme alike of the explorers and the philosophers of the period: "it was just being for a little while one of the 'prisca gens mortalium, the primitive race of men,' who ran about in the woods eating acorns and drinking water."[1] Boswell was as ill-fitted for the 'simple life' as he could be, but that does not impair the sincerity of the emotions which his Corsican travel aroused within him.

Moreover, the political condition of Corsica in 1765 had its own romantic attraction. The island was, as usual, in a state of revolt against the Republic of Genoa and the national cause was being upheld by one who was to become a Garibaldi of his own generation. Pasquale Paoli had been made

[1] p. 24 of this edition. See also Professor Tinker's Vanuxem Lectures, *Nature's Simple Plan* (1922).

General of the Corsicans in 1755 and had in a short time driven the Genoese "to the remotest corners of the island." The Genoese, failing to "allure the Corsicans to a pacifick submission," made a treaty with France by which certain towns were to be garrisoned by French troops. These troops, however, under the command of the Count de Marboeuf, acted only on the defensive and it was during this comparatively peaceful period of occupation that Boswell visited the island.

In Corsica, which Rousseau described as the one country still capable of legislation, Boswell found a people "actually fighting for liberty." "Europe," he writes, "now turns her eyes upon them, and with astonishment sees them on the eve of emancipating themselves for ever from a foreign yoke." *The London Chronicle* for 1766 is full of paragraphs (no doubt written or inspired by Boswell himself) advertising both the claims of Corsica and the importance of Boswell's tour: "Nothing," says a letter from Leghorn of 3 January, 1766, "can be a greater proof of the weak and desponding spirit of the Genoese than the apprehensions which Mr Boswell's tour to Corsica has occasioned"; "We are in great hopes," says a letter from Turin of 6 January, 1766, "that from what he has seen, he will be able to undeceive his countrymen with regard to the Corsican nation."

Boswell's book was no mean instrument in fanning the flame of enthusiasm for Paoli and his compatriots: Lord Lyttelton, Horace Walpole, Mrs Macaulay and David Garrick wrote him "noble letters" about it; Gray declared that Paoli was a man born two thousand years after his time; Mrs Barbauld wrote a poem on Corsica in which she celebrated

> ...the working thoughts which swelled the breast
> Of generous Boswell.

Nor was Boswell content with the writing of a single book. He supervised the publication of a volume of *British Essays in behalf of the Brave Corsicans*; he raised a subscription in Scotland; he preached the cause in Ireland; clad in the costume of a Corsican chief he made a striking appearance at the Shakespeare festival at Stratford-on-Avon in 1769, an event duly chronicled—by himself—in the *London Magazine*[1]; wearing the same costume, he sought, and obtained, an interview with Chatham. But it was to no purpose. Corsica was ceded to the French in 1769 and England was not sufficiently enthusiastic to intervene. "Foolish as we are," said Lord Holland, "we cannot be so foolish as to go to war because Mr Boswell has been in Corsica." Paoli resisted for a while and then took refuge in England, where he quickly became a *persona grata* in the Johnsonian circle.

But though the *Tour* has a definite place in the literature of travel, its real interest lies in its early exemplification of the literary qualities and methods of James Boswell.

He had begun to keep a journal as early as 1758

[1] See frontispiece.

and throughout his tour he was busy with his note-book, recording his impressions every night and afterwards making a selection at leisure. His Corsican adventures were begun under what were for him the most agreeable conditions. He was a figure; he provoked comment; he was thought to be engaged upon a political mission. With that exquisite sensitiveness to his surroundings which is one of his most engaging qualities, Boswell could, with complete sincerity, yearn for "the serenity and peace of mind to be found in convents"; he could acquit himself wittily and well in the rôle of Protestant apologist; he could lecture the Corsicans on the dangers of luxury and refinement; he could allow himself a "momentary pride" as he rode out on Paoli's horse, "with rich furniture of crimson velvet, with broad gold lace"; he could feel a supreme elevation of mind as Paoli argued for "the being and attributes of GOD"; he could fancy himself, as he sang his 'Cuore di quercia,' to be a recruiting-officer with his chorus of Corsicans aboard the British fleet.

Of the genuineness of these and other emotions there can be no question, and they are recorded with that unaffected good humour which made Boswell irresistible to his own, as to later, generations. Gray's verdict that the *Tour to Corsica* was an example of how "any fool may write a most valuable book by chance, if he will only tell us what he heard and saw with veracity," will not hold. On all Boswell's literary work there is the mark of the conscious artist; his sense of selection, as well as of composition, is sure; and the *Tour to Corsica* abounds in those vivid touches, both descriptive and introspective, with which readers of the *Life of Johnson* are familiar.

What could be more economical, or more effective, than Boswell's description of his servant: "an honest Swiss who loved to eat and drink well"? What more picturesque than the few lines about the little boy who ran to his mother to bring the great seal of the kingdom? What more engaging than the account of how the 'ambasciadore Inglese' got a Corsican dress made and walked about in it "with an air of true satisfaction"?

No wonder Boswell's gay ideas relaxed Paoli's severity and brightened up his humour.

"For my part," writes Boswell in his *Preface*, "I should be proud to be known as an authour . . . of all possessions I should imagine literary fame to be the most valuable."

Seldom has an ambition been so completely fulfilled; "I have obtained my desire" he was able to write in the *Preface* to the third edition, and it is high, but not extravagant, praise to say that the *Tour to Corsica* is not unworthy of the author of the *Life of Johnson*.

# NOTE ON THE TEXT

The text used for the present reprint is that of the third edition (1769), certain obvious misprints (including one in the quotation on the title-page) being corrected. A collation of the first and third editions has revealed the following variant readings in the former:

p. 4: footnote omitted.
p. 9, l. 7: *lay my account with instant death.*
p. 12, bottom: *advices.*
p. 18, bottom: *joked them with the text.*
p. 23, l. 1: *hath* omitted.
p. 27, l. 7: *droll enough.*
p. 37, l. 17: *I came in to pay.*
p. 62, l. 10: *the lively nobleman.*
p. 71, l. 6: *with a keenness.*
p. 91, l. 1: *Signor Buttafoco, who proved superiour to the character I had conceived of him from the letter of M. Rousseau. I found in him the incorrupted virtues of the brave islander, with the improvements of the continent. I found him in short, to be a man of principle, abilities and knowledge; and at the same time a man of the world. He is now deservedly raised to the rank of colonel of the Royal Corsicans, in the service of France. I past some days with Signor Buttafoco, from whose conversation I received so much pleasure, that I in a great measure forgot my ague.*
p. 102, l. 1: *a total expulsion.*

It will be observed that the only important

textual change arises from Boswell's revised esti-
mate of the qualities of Signor Buttafoco[1].

The very considerable differences in punctua-
tion have not been recorded, but what is more
interesting is Boswell's failure to carry out, *au pied
de la lettre*, his own explicit injunctions as to the
preservation of his original spelling.

"Of late," wrote Boswell in his *Preface*, "it has
become the fashion to render our language more
neat and trim by leaving out k after c, and u in
the last syllable of words which used to end in
our. . . . I have retained the k and . . . wherever a
word originally Latin has been transmitted to us
through the medium of the French, I have written
it with the characteristical u. . . . If this work should
at any future period be reprinted, I hope that care
will be taken of my orthography."

In spite of this, Boswell would appear to have
passed *domestic* (p. 42), *authentic* (p. 56), *legislator*
(p. 94), *public* (p. 108) in the proofs of the third
edition.

In the interests of consistency as well as of
fidelity to Boswell's intentions, it has seemed best
to restore the original forms of these and other
words (*risque, chearful, compleat*, etc.) in this reprint.

Finally, two small points with regard to the text
of the first edition may be noted: first, there are
two 'states' of this edition, since certain copies

[1] Fitzgerald's bibliographical note (*Life of Boswell*, II,
276), implying that the third edition corresponds page for
page with the first and second, is curiously inaccurate.

contain a misprint on p. 296[1] (*my own of* for *of my own*); secondly, the leaf Z 3 is a cancel. Professor Tinker, who has been fortunate enough to find the leaf in its original state, informs me that it is of little interest. It appears to have been cancelled in order to correct the spelling of 'Mariani.'[2]

[1] p. 33 in the present edition.
[2] p. 88 in the present edition.

THE

# J O U R N A L

OF A

# T O U R

TO

# C O R S I C A.

HAVING resolved to pass some years abroad, for my instruction and entertainment, I conceived a design of visiting the island of Corsica. I wished for something more than just the common course of what is called the tour of Europe; and Corsica occurred to me as a place which no body else had seen, and where I should find what was to be seen no where else, a people actually fighting for liberty, and forming themselves from a poor inconsiderable oppressed nation, into a flourishing and independent state.

When I got into Switzerland, I went to see M. Rousseau. He was then living in romantick retirement, from whence, perhaps, it had been better for him never to have descended. While he was at a distance, his singular eloquence filled our minds with high ideas of the wild philosopher. When he came into the walks of men, we know alas! how much these ideas suffered.

He entertained me very courteously; for I was recommended to him by my honoured friend the Earl Marischal, with whom I had the happiness of travelling through a part of Germany. I had heard that M. Rousseau had some correspondence with the Corsicans, and had been desired to assist them in forming their laws. I told him my scheme of going to visit them, after I had compleated my tour of Italy; and I insisted that he should give me a letter of introduction. He immediately agreed to do so, whenever I should acquaint him of my time of going thither; for he saw that my enthusiasm for the brave islanders was as warm as his own.

I accordingly wrote to him from Rome, in April 1765, that I had fixed the month of September for my Corsican expedition, and therefore begged of him to send me the letter of introduction, which if he refused, I should certainly go without it, and probably be hanged as a spy. So let him answer for the consequences.

The wild philosopher was a man of his word; and on my arrival at Florence in August, I received the following letter:

2

## A MONSIEUR, MONSIEUR BOSWELL, &c.

A Motiers, le 30 May, 1765.

' LA crise orageuse ou je me trouve, Monsieur,
' depuis votre depart d'ici, m'a oté le tems de re-
' pondre à votre premiére lettre, et me laisse à peine
' celui de repondre en peu de mots à la seconde.
' Pour m'en tenir à ce qui presse pour le moment,
' savoir la recommendation que vous desirez en
' Corse; puisque vous avez le desir de visiter ces
' braves insulaires, vous pourrez vous informer à
' Bastia, de M. Buttafoco capitaine au Regiment
' Royal Italien; il a sa maison à Vescovado, ou il
' se tient assez souvent. C'est un très-galant
' homme, qui a des connoissances et de l'esprit;
' il suffira de lui montrer cette lettre, et je suis sur
' qu'il vous recevra bien, et contribuera à vous faire
' voir l'isle et ses habitants avec satisfaction. Si
' vous ne trouvez pas M. Buttafoco, et que vous
' vouliez aller tout droit à M. Pascal de Paoli
' general de la nation, vous pouvez egalement lui
' montrer cette lettre, et je suis sur, connoissant la
' noblesse de son caractére, que vous serez très-
' content de son accueil: vous pourrez lui dire
' même que vous étes aimé de Mylord Mareschal
' d'Ecosse, et que Mylord Mareschal est un des

' plus zelés partizans de la nation Corse. Au reste
' vous n'avez besoin d'autre recommendation près
' de ces Messieurs que votre propre mérite, la
' nation Corse etant naturellement si accueillante
' et si hospitaliére, que tous les etrangers y sont
' bien venus et caressés.

*     *     *     *     *     *

' Bons et heureux voyages, santé, gaieté et
' promt retour. Je vous embrasse, Monsieur, de
' tout mon coeur

J. J. ROUSSEAU.

## To MR. BOSWELL, &c.

MOTIERS, the 30 May, 1765.

' THE stormy crisis in which I have found my-
' self, since your departure from this, has not
' allowed me any leisure to answer your first letter,
' and hardly allows me leisure to reply in a few
' words to your second. To confine myself to what
' is immediately pressing, the recommendation
' which you ask for Corsica; since you have a desire
' to visit those brave islanders, you may inquire
' at Bastia for M. Buttafoco*, captain of the Royal

---

* This man's plausibility imposed upon M. Rousseau
and me. But he has shewn himself to be mean and

4

'Italian Regiment; his house is at Vescovado,
'where he resides pretty often. He is a very worthy
'man, and has both knowledge and genius; it will
'be sufficient to shew him this letter, and I am sure
'he will receive you well, and will contribute to let
'you see the island and its inhabitants with satis-
'faction. If you do not find M. Buttafoco, and will
'go directly to M. Pascal Paoli General of the
'nation, you may in the same manner shew him
'this letter, and as I know the nobleness of his
'character, I am sure you will be very well pleased
'at your reception. You may even tell him that
'you are liked by My Lord Marischal of Scotland,
'and that My Lord Marischal is one of the most
'zealous partisans of the Corsican nation. You
'need no other recommendation to these gentle-
'men but your own merit, the Corsicans being
'naturally so courteous and hospitable, that all
'strangers who come among them, are made wel-
'come and caressed.

\*  \*  \*  \*  \*  \*

treacherous; having betrayed Casinca to the French; for
which his memory will ever be infamous. They who are
possessed of the former editions of this book, are intreated
to erase what I have said of him, first edit. pages 360 and
361 and second edit. pages 362 and 363.

' I wish you agreeable and fortunate travels,
' health, gaiety, and a speedy return. I embrace
' you, Sir, with all my heart

JOHN JAMES ROUSSEAU.


Furnished with these credentials, I was impatient
to be with the illustrious Chief. The charms of sweet
Siena detained me longer than they should have
done. I required the hardy air of Corsica to brace
me, after the delights of Tuscany.

I recollect with astonishment how little the real
state of Corsica was known, even by those who
had good access to know it. An officer of rank in
the British navy, who had been in several ports of
the island, told me that I run the risque of my life
in going among these barbarians; for, that his surgeon's mate went ashore to take the diversion of
shooting, and every moment was alarmed by some
of the natives, who started from the bushes with
loaded guns, and if he had not been protected by
Corsican guides, would have certainly blown out
his brains.

Nay at Leghorn, which is within a day's sailing
of Corsica, and has a constant intercourse with it,
I found people who dissuaded me from going
thither, because it might be dangerous.

6

I was however under no apprehension in going
to Corsica, Count Rivarola the Sardinian consul,
who is himself a Corsican, assuring me that the
island was then in a very civilized state; and besides,
that in the rudest times no Corsican would ever
attack a stranger. The Count was so good as to
give me most obliging letters to many people in
the island. I had now been in several foreign
countries. I had found that I was able to accom-
modate myself to my fellow-creatures of different
languages and sentiments. I did not fear that it
would be a difficult task for me to make myself
easy with the plain and generous Corsicans.

The only danger I saw was, that I might be
taken by some of the Barbary corsairs, and have
a tryal of slavery among the Turks at Algiers. I
spoke of it to commodore Harrison, who com-
manded the British squadron in the Mediterranean,
and was then lying with his ship the Centurion, in
the bay of Leghorn. He assured me, that if the
Turks did take me, they should not keep me long;
but in order to prevent it, he was so good as to
grant me a very ample and particular passport; and
as it could be of no use if I did not meet the corsairs,
he said very pleasantly when he gave it me, 'I hope,
Sir, it shall be of no use to you.'

Before I left Leghorn, I could observe, that my

tour was looked upon by the Italian politicians in a very serious light, as if truly I had a commission from my Court, to negotiate a treaty with the Corsicans. The more I disclaimed any such thing, the more they persevered in affirming it; and I was considered as a very close young man. I therefore just allowed them to make a minister of me, till time should undeceive them.

I sailed from Leghorn in a Tuscan vessel, which was going over to Capo Corso for wine. I preferred this to a vessel going to Bastia, because as I did not know how the French general was affected towards the Corsicans, I was afraid that he might not permit me to go forward to Paoli. I therefore resolved to land on the territories of the nation, and after I had been with the illustrious Chief, to pay my respects to the French if I should find it safe.

Though from Leghorn to Corsica, is usually but one day's sailing, there was so dead a calm that it took us two days. The first day was the most tedious. However there were two or three Corsicans aboard, and one of them played on the citra, which amused me a good deal. At sunset all the people in the ship sung the Ave Maria, with great devotion and some melody. It was pleasing to enter into the spirit of their religion, and hear them offering up their evening orisons.

The second day we became better acquainted, and more lively and chearful. The worthy Corsicans thought it was proper to give a moral lesson to a young traveller just come from Italy. They told me that in their country I should be treated with the greatest hospitality; but if I attempted to debauch any of their women, I might expect instant death.

I employed myself several hours in rowing, which gave me great spirits. I relished fully my approach to the island, which had acquired an unusual grandeur in my imagination. As long as I can remember any thing, I have heard of 'The ' malecontents of Corsica, with Paoli at their head.' It was a curious thought that I was just going to see them.

About seven o'clock at night, we landed safely in the harbour of Centuri. I learnt that Signor Giaccomini of this place, to whom I was recommended by Count Rivarola, was just dead. He had made a handsome fortune in the East Indies; and having had a remarkable warmth in the cause of liberty during his whole life, he shewed it in the strongest manner in his last will. He bequeathed a considerable sum of money, and some pieces of ordnance, to the nation. He also left it in charge to his heir, to live in Corsica, and be firm in the

9

patriotick interest; and if ever the island should again be reduced under the power of the Genoese, he ordered him to retire with all his effects to Leghorn. Upon these conditions only, could his heir enjoy his estate.

I was directed to the house of Signor Giaccomini's cousin, Signor Antonio Antonetti at Morfiglia, about a mile up the country. The prospect of the mountains covered with vines and olives, was extremely agreeable; and the odour of the myrtle and other aromatick shrubs and flowers that grew all around me, was very refreshing. As I walked along, I often saw Corsican peasants come suddenly out from the covert; and as they were all armed, I saw how the frightened imagination of the surgeon's mate had raised up so many assassins. Even the man who carried my baggage was armed, and had I been timorous might have alarmed me. But he and I were very good company to each other. As it grew dusky, I repeated to myself these lines from a fine passage in Ariosto:

> E pur per selve oscure e calli obliqui
> Insieme van, senza sospetto aversi.
>
> ARIOST. Canto I.

> Together through dark woods and winding ways
> They walk, nor on their hearts suspicion preys.

10

I delivered Signor Antonetti the letter for his deceased cousin. He read it, and received me with unaffected cordiality, making an apology for my frugal entertainment, but assuring me of a hearty welcome. His true kindly hospitality was also shewn in taking care of my servant, an honest Swiss, who loved to eat and drink well.

I had formed a strange notion that I should see every thing in Corsica totally different from what I had seen in any other country. I was therefore much surprised to find Signor Antonetti's house quite an Italian one, with very good furniture, prints, and copies of some of the famous pictures. In particular, I was struck to find here a small copy from Raphael, of St Michael and the Dragon. There was no necessity for its being well done. To see the thing at all was what surprised me.

Signor Antonetti gave me an excellent light repast, and a very good bed. He spoke with great strength of the patriotick cause, and with great veneration of the General. I was quite easy, and liked much the opening of my Corsican tour.

The next day, being Sunday, it rained very hard; and I must observe that the Corsicans with all their resolution, are afraid of bad weather, to a degree of effeminacy. I got indeed a droll but a just enough account of this, from one of them: 'Sir, said he, if

' you were as poor as a Corsican, and had but one
' coat, so as that after being wet, you could not put
' on dry cloaths, you would be afraid too.' Signor
Antonetti would not allow me to set out while it
rained, for, said he, 'Quando si trova fuori, patien-
' za; ma di andare fuori è cattivo. If a man finds
' himself abroad, there is no help for it. But to
' go deliberately out, is too much.'

When the day grew a little better, I accompanied Signor Antonetti and his family, to hear
mass in the parish church, a very pretty little
building, about half a quarter of a mile off.

Signor Antonetti's parish priest was to preach
to us, at which I was much pleased, being very
curious to hear a Corsican sermon.

Our priest did very well. His text was in the
Psalms: 'Descendunt ad infernum viventes. They
' go down alive into the pit.'

After endeavouring to move our passions with
a description of the horrours of hell, he told us,
' Saint Catharine of Siena wished to be laid on the
' mouth of this dreadful pit, that she might stop
' it up, so as no more unhappy souls should fall
' into it. I confess, my brethren, I have not the
' zeal of holy Saint Catharine. But I do what I
' can; I warn you how to avoid it.' He then gave
us some good practical advice, and concluded.

12

The weather being now cleared up, I took leave of the worthy gentleman to whom I had been a guest. He gave me a letter to Signor Damiano Tomasi, Padre del Commune at Pino, the next village. I got a man with an ass to carry my baggage. But such a road I never saw. It was absolutely scrambling along the face of a rock overhanging the sea, upon a path sometimes not above a foot broad. I thought the ass rather retarded me; so I prevailed with the man, to take my portmanteau and other things on his back.

Had I formed my opinion of Corsica from what I saw this morning, I might have been in as bad humour with it, as Seneca was, whose refleótions in prose are not inferiour to his epigrams: 'Quid ' tam nudum inveniri potest, quid tam abruptum ' undique quam hoc saxum? quid ad copias, respi- ' cienti jejunius? quid ad homines immansuetius? ' quid ad ipsum loci situm horridius? Plures tamen ' hîc peregrini quam cives consistunt? usque eò ' ergo commutatio ipsa locorum gravis non est, ut ' hic quoque locus a patria quosdam abduxerit (*a*). ' What can be found so bare, what so rugged all ' around as this rock? what more barren of pro- ' visions? what more rude as to its inhabitants?

(*a*) Seneca de Consolatione.

13

'what in the very situation of the place more
'horrible? what in climate more intemperate? yet
'there are more foreigners than natives here. So
'far then is a change of place from being disagree-
'able, that even this place hath brought some
'people away from their country.'

At Pino I was surprised to find myself met by
some brisk young fellows drest like English sailors,
and speaking English tolerably well. They had
been often with cargoes of wine at Leghorn, where
they had picked up what they knew of our language,
and taken clothes in part of payment for some of
their merchandise.

I was cordially entertained at Signor Tomasi's.
Throughout all Corsica, except in garrison towns,
there is hardly an inn. I met with a single one,
about eight miles from Corte. Before I was accustomed to the Corsican hospitality, I sometimes
forgot myself, and imagining I was in a publick
house, called for what I wanted, with the tone
which one uses in calling to the waiters at a tavern.
I did so at Pino, asking for a variety of things at
once; when Signora Tomasi perceiving my mistake, looked in my face and smiled, saying with
much calmness and good nature, 'Una cosa dopo
'un altra, Signore. One thing after another, Sir.'

In writing this Journal, I shall not tire my

readers, with relating the occurrences of each particular day. It will be much more agreeable to them, to have a free and continued account of what I saw or heard, most worthy of observation.

For some time, I had very curious travelling, mostly on foot, and attended by a couple of stout women, who carried my baggage upon their heads. Every time that I prepared to set out from a village, I could not help laughing, to see the good people eager to have my equipage in order, and roaring out, 'Le Donne, Le Donne. The Women, The Women.'

I had full leisure and the best opportunities to observe every thing, in my progress through the island. I was lodged sometimes in private houses, sometimes in convents, being always well recommended from place to place. The first convent in which I lay, was at Canari. It appeared a little odd at first. But I soon learnt to repair to my dormitory as naturally as if I had been a friar for seven years.

The convents were small decent buildings, suited to the sober ideas of their pious inhabitants. The religious who devoutly endeavour to 'walk with GOD,' are often treated with raillery, by those whom pleasure or business prevents from thinking of future and more exalted objects. A little experience of the serenity and peace of mind to be found in convents, would be of use to temper the fire of men of the world.

At Patrimonio I found the seat of a provincial magistracy. The chief judge was there, and entertained me very well. Upon my arrival, the captain of the guard came out, and demanded who I was? I replied 'Inglese, English.' He looked at me seriously, and then said in a tone between regret and upbraiding, 'Inglese, c'erano i nostri amici; ' ma non le sono più. The English; they were once ' our friends; but they are so no more.' I felt for my country, and was abashed before this honest soldier.

At Oletta I visited Count Nicholas Rivarola, brother to my friend at Leghorn. He received me with great kindness, and did every thing in his power to make me easy. I found here a Corsican who thought better of the British, than the captain of the guard at Patrimonio. He talked of our bombarding San Fiorenzo, in favour of the patriots, and willingly gave me his horse for the afternoon, which he said he would not have done to a man of any other nation.

When I came to Morato, I had the pleasure of being made acquainted with Signor Barbaggi, who is married to the niece of Paoli. I found him to be a sensible intelligent well-bred man. The mint of

16

Corsica was in his house. I got specimens of their different kinds of money in silver and copper and was told that they hoped in a year or two to strike some gold coins. Signor Barbaggi's house was repairing, so I was lodged in the convent. But in the morning returned to breakfast, and had chocolate; and at dinner we had no less than twelve well-drest dishes, served on Dresden china, with a desert, different sorts of wine, and a liqueur, all the produce of Corsica. Signor Barbaggi was frequently repeating to me, that the Corsicans inhabited a rude uncultivated country, and that they lived like Spartans. I begged leave to ask him in what country he could shew me greater luxury than I had seen in his house; and I said I should certainly tell wherever I went, what tables the Corsicans kept, notwithstanding their pretensions to poverty and temperance. A good deal of pleasantry passed upon this. His lady was a genteel woman, and appeared to be agreeable, though very reserved.

From Morato to Corte, I travelled through a wild mountainous rocky country, diversified with some large valleys. I got little beasts for me and my servant, sometimes horses, but oftener mules or asses. We had no bridles, but cords fixed round their necks, with which we managed them as well as we could.

At Corte I waited upon the supreme council, to one of whom, Signor Boccociampe, I had a letter from Signor Barbaggi. I was very politely received, and was conducted to the Franciscan convent, where I got the apartment of Paoli, who was then some days journey beyond the mountains, holding a court of syndicato at a village called Sollacarò.

As the General resided for some time in this convent, the fathers made a better appearance than any I saw in the island. I was principally attended by the Priour, a resolute divine, who had formerly been in the army, and by Padre Giulio, a man of much address, who still favours me with his correspondence.

These fathers have a good vineyard and an excellent garden. They have between 30 and 40 beehives in long wooden cases or trunks of trees, with a covering of the bark of the cork tree. When they want honey, they burn a little juniper-wood, the smoak of which makes the bees retire. They then take an iron instrument with a sharp-edged crook at one end of it, and bring out the greatest part of the honey-comb, leaving only a little for the bees, who work the case full again. By taking the honey in this way, they never kill a bee. They seemed much at their ease, living in peace and plenty. I often joked with them on the text which

18

is applied to their order: 'Nihil habentes et omnia
' possidentes, Having nothing, and yet possessing
' all things.'

I went to the choir with them. The service was
conducted with propriety, and Padre Giulio played
on the organ. On the great altar of their church is
a tabernacle carved in wood by a Religious. It is a
piece of exquisite workmanship. A Genoese gentleman offered to give them one in silver for it; but
they would not make the exchange.

These fathers have no library worth mentioning;
but their convent is large and well built. I looked
about with great attention, to see if I could find any
inscriptions; but the only one I found was upon
a certain useful edifice:

> Sine necessitate huc non intrate,
> Quia necessaria sumus.

A studied, rhiming, Latin conceit marked upon
such a place was truly ludicrous.

I chose to stop a while at Corte, to repose myself
after my fatigues, and to see every thing about the
capital of Corsica.

The morning after my arrival here, three French
deserters desired to speak with me. The foolish
fellows had taken it into their heads, that I was
come to raise recruits for Scotland, and so they
begged to have the honour of going along with me;

I suppose with intention to have the honour of running off from me, as they had done from their own regiments.

I received many civilities at Corte from Signor Boccociampe, and from Signor Massesi the Great Chancellor, whose son Signor Luigi a young gentleman of much vivacity, and natural politeness, was so good as to attend me constantly as my conductour. I used to call him my governour. I liked him much, for as he had never been out of the island, his ideas were entirely Corsican.

Such of the members of the supreme council as were in residence during my stay at Corte, I found to be solid and sagacious, men of penetration and ability, well calculated to assist the General in forming his political plans, and in turning to the best advantage, the violence and enterprises of the people.

The university was not then sitting, so I could only see the rooms, which were shewn me by the Abbé Valentini, procuratour of the university. The professours were all absent except one Capuchin father whom I visited at his convent. It is a tolerable building, with a pretty large collection of books. There is in the church here a tabernacle carved in wood, in the manner of that at the Franciscans, but much inferiour to it.

I went up to the castle of Corte. The commandant very civilly shewed me every part of it. As I wished to see all things in Corsica, I desired to see even the unhappy criminals. There were then three in the castle; a man for the murder of his wife; a married lady who had hired one of her servants to strangle a woman of whom she was jealous; and the servant who had actually perpetrated this barbarous action. They were brought out from their cells, that I might talk with them. The murderer of his wife had a stupid hardened appearance, and told me he did it at the instigation of the devil. The servant was a poor despicable wretch. He had at first accused his mistress, but was afterwards prevailed with to deny his accusation, upon which he was put to the torture, by having lighted matches held between his fingers. This made him return to what he had formerly said, so as to be a strong evidence against his mistress. His hands were so miserably scorched, that he was a piteous object. I asked him why he had committed such a crime, he said, 'Perche era senza spirito, Because I was without understanding.' The lady seemed of a bold and resolute spirit. She spoke to me with great firmness, and denied her guilt, saying with a contemptuous smile, as she pointed to her servant, 'They can force that creature to say what they please.'

21

The hangman of Corsica was a great curiosity. Being held in the utmost detestation, he durst not live like another inhabitant of the island. He was obliged to take refuge in the castle, and there he was kept in a little corner turret, where he had just room for a miserable bed, and a little bit of fire to dress such victuals for himself as were sufficient to keep him alive; for nobody would have any intercourse with him, but all turned their backs upon him. I went up and looked at him. And a more dirty rueful spectacle I never beheld. He seemed sensible of his situation, and held down his head like an abhorred outcast.

It was a long time before they could get a hangman in Corsica, so that the punishment of the gallows was hardly known, all their criminals being shot. At last this creature whom I saw, who is a Sicilian, came with a message to Paoli. The General who has a wonderful talent for physiognomy, on seeing the man, said immediately to some of the people about him, 'Ecco il boia, Behold our hangman.' He gave orders to ask the man if he would accept of the office, and his answer was, 'My grandfather was a hangman, my father was a hangman. I have been a hangman myself, and am willing to continue so.' He was therefore immediately put into office, and the ignominious death dispensed by his hands, hath had more effect than twenty executions by fire arms.

It is remarkable that no Corsican would upon any account consent to be hangman. Not the greatest criminals, who might have had their lives upon that condition. Even the wretch, who for a paultry hire, had strangled a woman, would rather submit to death, than do the same action, as the executioner of the law.

When I had seen every thing about Corte, I prepared for my journey over the mountains, that I might be with Paoli. The night before I set out, I recollected that I had forgotten to get a passport, which, in the present situation of Corsica, is still a necessary precaution. After supper therefore the Priour walked with me to Corte, to the house of the Great Chancellor, who ordered the passport to be made out immediately, and while his secretary was writing it, entertained me by reading to me some of the minutes of the general consulta. When the passport was finished, and ready to have the seal put to it, I was much pleased with a beautiful, simple incident. The Chancellor desired a little boy who was playing in the room by us, to run to his mother, and bring the great seal of the kingdom. I thought myself sitting in the house of a Cincinnatus.

Next morning I set out in very good order, having excellent mules, and active clever Corsican guides. The worthy fathers of the convent who treated me in the kindest manner while I was their guest, would also give me some provisions for my journey; so they put up a gourd of their best wine, and some delicious pomegranates. My Corsican guides appeared so hearty, that I often got down and walked along with them, doing just what I saw them do. When we grew hungry, we threw stones among the thick branches of the chestnut trees which overshadowed us, and in that manner we brought down a shower of chestnuts with which we filled our pockets, and went on eating them with great relish; and when this made us thirsty, we lay down by the side of the first brook, put our mouths to the stream, and drank sufficiently. It was just being for a little while, one of the 'prisca gens mortalium, the primitive race of men,' who ran about in the woods eating acorns and drinking water.

While I stopped to refresh my mules at a little village, the inhabitants came crouding about me as an ambassadour going to their General. When they were informed of my country, a strong black fellow among them said, 'Inglese! sono barbari; ' non credono in Dio grande. English! they are

' barbarians; they don't believe in the great God.'
I told him, Excuse me, Sir. We do believe in GOD,
and in Jesus Christ too. 'Um, said he, e nel Papa?
' and in the Pope?' No. 'E perche? And why?'
This was a puzzling question in these circumstances; for there was a great audience to the con-
troversy. I thought I would try a method of my
own, and very gravely replied, 'Perche siamo
' troppo lontani. Because we are too far off.' A
very new argument against the universal infalli-
bility of the Pope. It took however; for my opponent
mused a while, and then said, 'Troppo lontani!
' La Sicilia è tanto lontana che l'Inghilterra; e in
' Sicilia si credono nel Papa. Too far off! Why
' Sicily is as far off as England. Yet in Sicily they
' believe in the Pope. O, said I, noi siamo dieci
' volte più lontani che la Sicilia! We are ten times
' farther off than Sicily. Aha!' said he; and seemed
quite satisfied. In this manner I got off very well.
I question much whether any of the learned
reasonings of our protestant divines would have
had so good an effect.

My journey over the mountains was very entertaining. I past some immense ridges and vast
woods. I was in great health and spirits, and fully
able to enter into the ideas of the brave rude men
whom I found in all quarters.

At Bastelica where there is a stately spirited race of people, I had a large company to attend me in the convent. I liked to see their natural frankness and ease; for why should men be afraid of their own species? They just came in making an easy bow, placed themselves round the room where I was sitting, rested themselves on their muskets, and immediately entered into conversation with me. They talked very feelingly of the miseries that their country had endured, and complained that they were still but in a state of poverty. I happened at that time to have an unusual flow of spirits; and as one who finds himself amongst utter strangers in a distant country, has no timidity, I harangued the men of Bastelica with great fluency. I expatiated on the bravery of the Corsicans, by which they had purchased liberty, the most valuable of all possessions, and rendered themselves glorious over all Europe. Their poverty, I told them, might be remedied by a proper cultivation of their island, and by engaging a little in commerce. But I bid them remember, that they were much happier in their present state than in a state of refinement and vice; and that therefore they should beware of luxury.

What I said had the good fortune to touch them, and several of them repeated the same sentiments

much better than I could do. They all expressed
their strong attachment to Paoli, and called out in
one voice that they were all at his command. I
could with pleasure, have passed a long time here.

At Ornano I saw the ruins of the seat where the
great Sampiero had his residence. They were a
pretty droll society of monks in the convent at
Ornano. When I told them that I was an English-
man, 'Aye, aye, said one of them, as was well
' observed by a reverend bishop, when talking of
' your pretended reformation, Angli olim angeli
' nunc diaboli. The English formerly angels now
' devils.' I looked upon this as an honest effusion
of spiritual zeal. The fathers took good care of me
in temporals.

When I at last came within sight of Sollacarò,
where Paoli was, I could not help being under
considerable anxiety. My ideas of him had been
greatly heightened by the conversations I had held
with all sorts of people in the island, they having
represented him to me as something above humanity. I had the strongest desire to see so exalted a
character; but I feared that I should be unable to
give a proper account why I had presumed to
trouble him with a visit, and that I should sink to
nothing before him. I almost wished yet to go back
without seeing him. These workings of sensibility

employed my mind till I rode through the village, and came up to the house where he was lodged.

Leaving my servant with my guides, I past through the guards, and was met by some of the General's people, who conducted me into an anti-chamber, where were several gentlemen in waiting. Signor Boccociampe had notified my arrival, and I was shewn into Paoli's room. I found him alone, and was struck with his appearance. He is tall, strong, and well made; of a fair complexion, a sensible, free, and open countenance, and a manly, and noble carriage. He was then in his fortieth year. He was drest in green and gold. He used to wear the common Corsican habit, but on the arrival of the French, he thought a little external elegance might be of use, to make the government appear in a more respectable light.

He asked me what were my commands for him. I presented him a letter from count Rivarola, and when he had read it, I shewed him my letter from Rousseau. He was polite, but very reserved. I had stood in the presence of many a prince, but I never had such a trial as in the presence of Paoli. I have already said, that he is a great physiognomist. In consequence of his being in continual danger from treachery and assassination, he has formed a habit of studiously observing every new face. For ten

28

minutes we walked backwards and forwards through the room, hardly saying a word, while he looked at me, with a stedfast, keen and penetrating eye, as if he searched my very soul.

This interview was for a while very severe upon me. I was much relieved when his reserve wore off, and he began to speak more. I then ventured to address him with this compliment to the Corsicans: ' Sir, I am upon my travels, and have lately visited ' Rome. I am come from seeing the ruins of one ' brave and free people: I now see the rise of ' another.'

He received my compliment very graciously; but observed that the Corsicans had no chance of being like the Romans, a great conquering nation, who should extend its empire over half the globe. Their situation, and the modern political systems, rendered this impossible. But, said he, Corsica may be a very happy country.

He expressed a high admiration of M. Rousseau, whom Signor Buttafoco had invited to Corsica, to aid the nation in forming its laws.

It seems M. de Voltaire had reported, in his rallying manner, that the invitation was merely a trick which he had put upon Rousseau. Paoli told me that when he understood this, he himself wrote to Rousseau, enforcing the invitation. Of this affair

I shall give a full account in an after part of my Journal.

Some of the nobles who attended him, came into the room, and in a little we were told that dinner was served up. The General did me the honour to place me next him. He had a table of fifteen or sixteen covers, having always a good many of the principal men of the island with him. He had an Italian cook who had been long in France; but he chose to have a few plain substantial dishes, avoiding every kind of luxury, and drinking no foreign wine.

I felt myself under some constraint in such a circle of heroes. The General talked a great deal on history and on literature. I soon perceived that he was a fine classical scholar, that his mind was enriched with a variety of knowledge, and that his conversation at meals was instructive and entertaining. Before dinner he had spoken French. He now spoke Italian, in which he is very eloquent.

We retired to another room to drink coffee. My timidity wore off. I no longer anxiously thought of myself; my whole attention was employed in listening to the illustrious commander of a nation.

He recommended me to the care of the Abbé Rostini, who had lived many years in France. Signor Colonna, the lord of the manor here, being from home, his house was assigned for me to live in. I was left by myself till near supper time, when I returned to the General, whose conversation improved upon me, as did the society of those about him, with whom I gradually formed an acquaintance.

Every day I felt myself happier. Particular marks of attention were shewn me as a subject of Great Britain, the report of which went over to Italy, and confirmed the conjectures that I was really an envoy. In the morning I had my chocolate served up upon a silver salver adorned with the arms of Corsica. I dined and supped constantly with the General. I was visited by all the nobility, and whenever I chose to make a little tour, I was attended by a party of guards. I begged of the General not to treat me with so much ceremony; but he insisted upon it.

One day when I rode out, I was mounted on Paoli's own horse, with rich furniture of crimson velvet, with broad gold lace, and had my guards marching along with me. I allowed myself to indulge a momentary pride in this parade, as I was curious to experience what could really be the pleasure of state and distinction with which mankind are so strangely intoxicated.

When I returned to the continent after all this

greatness, I used to joke with my acquaintance, and tell them that I could not bear to live with them, for they did not treat me with a proper respect.

My time passed here in the most agreeable manner. I enjoyed a sort of luxury of noble sentiment. Paoli became more affable with me. I made myself known to him. I forgot the great distance between us, and had every day some hours of private conversation with him.

From my first setting out on this tour, I wrote down every night what I had observed during the day, throwing together a great deal, that I might afterwards make a selection at leisure.

Of these particulars, the most valuable to my readers, as well as to myself, must surely be the memoirs and remarkable sayings of Paoli, which I am proud to record.

Talking of the Corsican war, 'Sir, said he, if the event prove happy, we shall be called great defenders of liberty. If the event shall prove unhappy, we shall be called unfortunate rebels.'

The French objected to him that the Corsican nation had no regular troops. We would not have them, said Paoli. We should then have the bravery of this and the other regiment. At present every single man is as a regiment himself. Should the

Corsicans be formed into regular troops, we should lose that personal bravery which has produced such actions among us, as in another country would have rendered famous even a Marischal.

I asked him how he could possibly have a soul so superiour to interest. 'It is not superiour, said he; my interest is to gain a name. I know well that he who does good to his country will gain that: and I expect it. Yet could I render this people happy, I would be content to be forgotten. I have an unspeakable pride, "Una superbia indicible." The approbation of my own heart is enough.'

He said he would have great pleasure in seeing the world, and enjoying the society of the learned and the accomplished in every country. I asked him how with these dispositions, he could bear to be confined to an island yet in a rude uncivilized state; and instead of participating Attick evenings, 'noctes coenaeque Deûm,' be in a continual course of care and of danger. He replied in one line of Virgil:

Vincet amor patriae laudumque immensa cupido.

This uttered with the fine open Italian pronunciation, and the graceful dignity of his manner, was very noble. I wished to have a statue of him taken at that moment.

I asked him if he understood English. He immediately began and spoke it, which he did tolerably well. When at Naples, he had known several Irish gentlemen who were officers in that service. Having a great facility in acquiring languages, he learnt English from them. But as he had been now ten years without ever speaking it, he spoke very slow. One could see that he was possessed of the words, but for want of what I may call mechanical practice, he had a difficulty in expressing himself.

I was diverted with his English library. It consisted of

Some broken volumes of the Spectatour and Tattler.

Pope's Essay on Man.

Gulliver's Travels.

A History of France, in old English.

And

Barclay's Apology for the Quakers.

I promised to send him some English books*.

* I have sent him the Works of Harrington, of Sidney, of Addison, of Trenchard, of Gordon, and of other writers in favour of liberty. I have also sent him some of our best books of morality and entertainment, in particular the Works of Mr. Samuel Johnson, with a compleat set of the Spectatour, Tattler and Guardian; and to the University of Corte, I have sent a few of the Greek and Roman Classicks, of the beautiful editions of the Messieurs Foulis at Glasgow.

He convinced me how well he understood our language; for I took the liberty to shew him a Memorial which I had drawn up on the advantages to Great Britain from an alliance with Corsica, and he translated this memorial into Italian with the greatest facility. He has since given me more proofs of his knowledge of our tongue by his answers to the letters which I have had the honour to write to him in English, and in particular by a very judicious and ingenious criticism on some of Swift's works.

He was well acquainted with the history of Britain. He had read many of the parliamentary debates, and had even seen a number of the North Briton. He shewed a considerable knowledge of this country, and often introduced anecdotes and drew comparisons and allusions from Britain.

He said his great object was to form the Corsicans in such a manner that they might have a firm constitution, and might be able to subsist without him. 'Our state, said he, is young, and still requires the leading strings. I am desirous that the Corsicans should be taught to walk of themselves. Therefore when they come to me to ask whom they should choose for their Padre del Commune, or other Magistrate, I tell them, You know better than I do, the able and honest men among your neighbours. Consider the consequence of your choice, not only to yourselves in particular, but to the island in general. In this manner I accustom them to feel their own importance as members of the state.'

After representing the severe and melancholy state of oppression under which Corsica had so long groaned, he said, 'We are now to our country like the prophet Elishah stretched over the dead child of the Shunamite, eye to eye, nose to nose, mouth to mouth. It begins to recover warmth, and to revive. I hope it shall yet regain full health and vigour.'

I said that things would make a rapid progress, and that we should soon see all the arts and sciences flourish in Corsica. 'Patience, Sir, said he. If you saw a man who had fought a hard battle, who was much wounded, who was beaten to the ground, and who with difficulty could lift himself up, it would not be reasonable to ask him to get his hair well drest, and to put on embroidered clothes. Corsica has fought a hard battle, has been much wounded, has been beaten to the ground, and with difficulty can lift herself up. The arts and sciences are like dress and ornament. You cannot expect them from us for some time. But come back twenty or thirty years hence, and we'll shew you arts and

sciences, and concerts and assemblies, and fine
ladies, and we'll make you fall in love among us, Sir.'

He smiled a good deal, when I told him that
I was much surprised to find him so amiable, accomplished, and polite; for although I knew I was
to see a great man, I expected to find a rude
character, an Attila king of the Goths, or a Luit-
prand king of the Lombards.

I observed that although he had often a placid
smile upon his countenance, he hardly ever laughed.
Whether loud laughter in general society be a sign
of weakness or rusticity, I cannot say; but I have
remarked that real great men, and men of finished
behaviour, seldom fall into it.

The variety, and I may say versatility, of the
mind of this great man is amazing. One day when
I came to pay my respects to him before dinner,
I found him in much agitation, with a circle of
his nobles around him, and a Corsican standing
before him like a criminal before his judge. Paoli
immediately turned to me, 'I am glad you are
come, Sir. You protestants talk much against our
doctrine of transubstantiation. Behold here the
miracle of transubstantiation, a Corsican tran-
substantiated into a Genoese. That unworthy man
who now stands before me is a Corsican, who has
been long a lieutenant under the Genoese, in Capo

Corso. Andrew Doria and all their greatest heroes could not be more violent for the republick than he has been, and all against his country.' Then turning to the man, 'Sir, said he, Corsica makes it a rule to pardon the most unworthy of her children, when they surrender themselves, even when they are forced to do so, as is your case. You have now escaped. But take care. I shall have a strict eye upon you; and if ever you make the least attempt to return to your traiterous practices, you know I can be avenged of you.' He spoke this with the fierceness of a lion, and from the awful darkness of his brow, one could see that his thoughts of vengeance were terrible. Yet when it was over, he all at once resumed his usual appearance, called out 'andiamo, come along;' went to dinner, and was as cheerful and gay as if nothing had happened.

His notions of morality are high and refined, such as become the Father of a nation. Were he a libertine, his influence would soon vanish; for men will never trust the important concerns of society to one they know will do what is hurtful to society for his own pleasures. He told me that his father had brought him up with great strictness, and that he had very seldom deviated from the paths of virtue. That this was not from a defect of feeling and passion, but that his mind being filled with important objects, his passions were employed in more noble pursuits than those of licentious pleasure. I saw from Paoli's example the great art of preserving young men of spirit from the contagion of vice, in which there is often a species of sentiment, ingenuity and enterprise nearly allied to virtuous qualities.

Shew a young man that there is more real spirit in virtue than in vice, and you have a surer hold of him, during his years of impetuosity and passion, than by convincing his judgement of all the rectitude of ethicks.

One day at dinner, he gave us the principal arguments for the being and attributes of GOD. To hear these arguments repeated with graceful energy by the illustrious Paoli in the midst of his heroick nobles, was admirable. I never felt my mind more elevated.

I took occasion to mention the king of Prussia's infidel writings, and in particular his epistle to Marischal Keith. Paoli who often talks with admiration of the greatness of that monarch, instead of uttering any direct censure of what he saw to be wrong in so distinguished a hero, paused a little, and then said with a grave and most expressive look, 'C'est une belle consolation pour un vieux ' general mourant, "En peu de tems vous ne serez

' plus." It is fine consolation for an old general
' when dying, "In a little while you shall be no
" more."

He observed that the Epicurean philosophy
had produced but one exalted charaćter, whereas
Stoicism had been the seminary of great men.
What he now said put me in mind of these noble
lines of Lucan:

> Hi mores, haec duri immota Catonis
> Sećta fuit, servare modum finemque tenere,
> Naturamque sequi, patriaeque impendere vitam,
> Nec sibi sed toti genitum se credere mundo.
>
> LUCAN. Pharsal. lib. ii. l. 380.

> These were the strićter manners of the man,
> And this the stubborn course in which they ran;
> The golden mean unchanging to pursue,
> Constant to keep the purpos'd end in view;
> Religiously to follow nature's laws,
> And die with pleasure in his country's cause.
> To think he was not for himself design'd,
> But born to be of use to all mankind.
>
> ROWE.

When he was asked if he would quit the island
of which he had undertaken the protećtion, supposing a foreign power should create him a
Marischal, and make him governour of a province;
he replied, 'I hope they will believe I am more
honest, or more ambitious; for, said he, to accept

40

of the highest offices under a foreign power would be to serve.'

'To have been a colonel, a general or a marischal, said he, would have been sufficient for my table, for my taste in dress, for the beauty whom my rank would have entitled me to attend. But it would not have been sufficient for this spirit, for this imagination.' Putting his hand upon his bosom.

He reasoned one day in the midst of his nobles whether the commander of a nation should be married or not. 'If he is married, said he, there is a risk that he may be distracted by private affairs, and swayed too much by a concern for his family. If he is unmarried, there is a risk that not having the tender attachments of a wife and children, he may sacrifice all to his own ambition.' When I said he ought to marry and have a son to succeed him, 'Sir, said he, what security can I have that my son will think and act as I do? What sort of a son had Cicero, and what had Marcus Aurelius?'

He said to me one day when we were alone, 'I never will marry. I have not the conjugal virtues. Nothing would tempt me to marry, but a woman who should bring me an immense dowry, with which I might assist my country.'

But he spoke much in praise of marriage, as an institution which the experience of ages had found to be the best calculated for the happiness of individuals, and for the good of society. Had he been a private gentleman, he probably would have married, and I am sure would have made as good a husband and father as he does a supreme magistrate and a general. But his arduous and critical situation would not allow him to enjoy domestick felicity. He is wedded to his country, and the Corsicans are his children.

He often talked to me of marriage, told me licentious pleasures were delusive and transient, that I should never be truly happy till I was married, and that he hoped to have a letter from me soon after my return home, acquainting him that I had followed his advice, and was convinced from experience, that he was in the right. With such an engaging condescention did this great man behave to me. If I could but paint his manner, all my readers would be charmed with him.

He has a mind fitted for philosophical speculations as well as for affairs of state. One evening at supper, he entertained us for some time with some curious reveries and conjectures as to the nature of the intelligence of beasts, with regard to which, he observed human knowledge was as yet very imperfect. He in particular seemed fond of inquiring into the language of the brute creation.

He observed that beasts fully communicate their ideas to each other, and that some of them, such as dogs, can form several articulate sounds. In different ages there have been people who pretended to understand the language of birds and beasts. 'Perhaps, said Paoli, in a thousand years we may know this as well as we know things which appeared much more difficult to be known.' I have often since this conversation, indulged myself in such reveries. If it were not liable to ridicule, I would say that an acquaintance with the language of beasts would be a most agreeable acquisition to man, as it would enlarge the circle of his social intercourse.

On my return to Britain, I was disappointed to find nothing upon this subject in Doctour Gregory's Comparative View of the State and Faculties of Man with those of the Animal World, which was then just published. My disappointment however was in a good measure made up, by a picture of society, drawn by that ingenious and worthy authour, which may be well applied to the Corsicans: 'There is a ' certain period in the progress of society in which ' mankind appear to the greatest advantage. In ' this period, they have the bodily powers, and all ' the animal functions remaining in full vigour. ' They are bold, active, steady, ardent in the love

' of liberty and their native country. Their manners
' are simple, their social affections warm, and
' though they are greatly influenced by the ties of
' blood, yet they are generous and hospitable to
' strangers. Religion is universally regarded among
' them, though disguised by a variety of super-
' stitions (*a*).'

Paoli was very desirous that I should study the
character of the Corsicans. 'Go among them, said
he, the more you talk with them, you will do me
the greater pleasure. Forget the meanness of their
apparel. Hear their sentiments. You will find
honour, and sense and abilities among these poor
men.'

His heart grew big when he spoke of his countrymen. His own great qualities appeared to unusual
advantage, while he described the virtues of those
for whose happiness his whole life was employed.
'If, said he, I should lead into the field an army of
Corsicans against an army double their number,
let me speak a few words to the Corsicans, to
remind them of the honour of their country and
of their brave forefathers, I do not say that they
would conquer, but I am sure that not a man of
them would give way. The Corsicans, said he,
have a steady resolution that would amaze you.

(*a*) Preface to Comparative view, p. 8.

I wish you could see one of them die. It is a proverb among the Genoese, "I Corsi meritano la furca e la sanno soffrire. The Corsicans deserve the gallows, and they fear not to meet it." There is a real compliment to us in this saying.'

He told me, that in Corsica, criminals are put to death four and twenty hours after sentence is pronounced against them. 'This, said he, may not be over catholick, but it is humane.'

He went on and gave me several instances of the Corsican spirit.

'A sergeant, said he, who fell in one of our desperate actions, when just a-dying, wrote to me thus: "I salute you. Take care of my aged father. In two hours I shall be with the rest who have bravely died for their country."

'A Corsican gentleman who had been taken prisoner by the Genoese, was thrown into a dark dungeon, where he was chained to the ground. While he was in this dismal situation, the Genoese sent a message to him, that if he would accept of a commission in their service, he might have it. 'No, said he. Were I to accept of your offer, it ' would be with a determined purpose to take the ' first opportunity of returning to the service of my ' country. But I will not accept of it. For I would ' not have my countrymen even suspect that I 'could be one moment unfaithful.' And he remained in his dungeon.' Paoli went on: 'I defy Rome, Sparta or Thebes to shew me thirty years of such patriotism as Corsica can boast. Though the affection between relations is exceedingly strong in the Corsicans, they will give up their nearest relations for the good of their country, and sacrifice such as have deserted to the Genoese.'

He gave me a noble instance of a Corsican's feeling and greatness of mind: 'A criminal, said he, was condemned to die. His nephew came to me with a lady of distinction, that she might solicit his pardon. The nephew's anxiety made him think that the lady did not speak with sufficient force and earnestness. He therefore advanced, and addressed himself to me: "Sir, is it proper for me to " speak?" as if he felt that it was unlawful to make such an application. I bid him go on. "Sir, said " he with the deepest concern, may I beg the life " of my uncle? If it is granted, his relations will " make a gift to the state of a thousand zechins. " We will furnish fifty soldiers in pay during the " siege of Furiani. We will agree that my uncle " shall be banished, and will engage that he shall " never return to the island." I knew the nephew to be a man of worth, and I answered him. You are acquainted with the circumstances of this case.

Such is my confidence in you, that if you will say that giving your uncle a pardon would be just, useful or honourable for Corsica, I promise you it shall be granted. He turned about, burst into tears, and left me, saying, "Non vorei vendere " l'onore della patria per mille zechini. I would " not have the honour of our country sold for a " thousand zechins." And his uncle suffered.'

Although the General was one of the constituent members of the court of syndicato, he seldom took his chair. He remained in his own apartment; and if any of those whose suits were determined by the syndicato were not pleased with the sentence, they had an audience of Paoli, who never failed to convince them that justice had been done them. This appeared to me a necessary indulgence in the infancy of government. The Corsicans having been so long in a state of anarchy, could not all at once submit their minds to the regular authority of justice. They would submit implicitly to Paoli, because they love and venerate him. But such a submission is in reality being governed by their passions. They submit to one for whom they have a personal regard. They cannot be said to be perfectly civilized till they submit to the determinations of their magistrates as officers of the state, entrusted with the administration of justice. By convincing them that the magistrates judge with abilities and uprightness, Paoli accustoms the Corsicans to have that salutary confidence in their rulers, which is necessary for securing respect and stability to the government.

After having said much in praise of the Corsicans, 'Come, said he, you shall have a proof of what I tell you. There is a crowd in the next room, waiting for admittance to me. I will call in the first I see, and you shall hear him.' He who chanced to present himself, was a venerable old man. The General shook him by the hand, and bid him good day, with an easy kindness that gave the aged peasant full encouragement to talk to his Excellency with freedom. Paoli bid him not mind me, but say on. The old man then told him that there had been an unlucky tumult in the village where he lived, and that two of his sons were killed. That looking upon this as a heavy misfortune, but without malice on the part of those who deprived him of his sons, he was willing to have allowed it to pass without inquiry. But his wife anxious for revenge, had made an application to have them apprehended and punished. That he gave his Excellency this trouble to intreat that the greatest care might be taken, lest in the heat of enmity among his neighbours, any body should be punished as guilty of the blood of his sons, who was really innocent of it. There was something so generous in this sentiment, while at the same time the old man seemed full of grief for the loss of his children, that it touched my heart in the most sensible manner. Paoli looked at me with complacency and a kind of amiable triumph on the behaviour of the old man, who had a flow of words and a vivacity of gesture which fully justified what Petrus Cyrnaeus hath said of the Corsican eloquence: 'Diceres omnes esse bonos causidicos. 'You would say they are all good pleaders.'

I found Paoli had reason to wish that I should talk much with his countrymen, as it gave me a higher opinion both of him and of them. Thuanus has justly said, 'Sunt mobilia Corsorum ingenia. 'The dispositions of the Corsicans are changeable.' Yet after ten years, their attachment to Paoli is as strong as at the first. Nay, they have an enthusiastick admiration of him. 'Questo grand' uomo 'mandato per Dio a liberare la patria, This great 'man whom God hath sent to free our country,' was the manner in which they expressed themselves to me concerning him.

Those who attended on Paoli were all men of sense and abilities in their different departments. Some of them had been in foreign service. One of them, Signor Suzzoni, had been long in Germany. He spoke German to me, and recalled to my mind, the happy days which I have past among that plain, honest, brave people, who of all nations in the world, receive strangers with the greatest cordiality. Signor Gian Quilico Casa Bianca, of the most ancient Corsican nobility, was much my friend. He instructed me fully with regard to the Corsican government. He had even the patience to sit by me while I wrote down an account of it, which from conversations with Paoli, I afterwards enlarged and improved. I received many civilities from the Abbé Rostini, a man of literature, and distinguished no less for the excellency of his heart. His saying of Paoli deserves to be remembered: 'Nous ne craignons pas que notre General ' nous trompe ni qu'il se laisse tromper, We are ' not afraid that our General will deceive us, nor ' that he will let himself be deceived.'

I also received civilities from Father Guelfucci of the order of Servites, a man whose talents and virtues, united with a singular decency and sweetness of manners, have raised him to the honourable station of secretary to the General. Indeed all the gentlemen here behaved to me in the most obliging manner. We walked, rode, and went a-shooting together.

The peasants and soldiers were all frank, open,

lively and bold, with a certain roughness of manner which agrees well with their character, and is far from being displeasing. The General gave me an admirable instance of their plain and natural, solid good sense. A young French Marquis, very rich and very vain, came over to Corsica. He had a sovereign contempt for the barbarous inhabitants, and strutted about (andava a passo misurato) with prodigious airs of consequence. The Corsicans beheld him with a smile of ridicule, and said, 'Let him alone, he is young.'

The Corsican peasants and soldiers are very fond of baiting cattle with the large mountain dogs. This keeps up a ferocity among them which totally extinguishes fear. I have seen a Corsican in the very heat of a baiting, run in, drive off the dogs, seize the half-frantick animal by the horns, and lead it away. The common people did not seem much given to diversions. I observed some of them in the great hall of the house of Colonna where I was lodged, amusing themselves with playing at a sort of draughts in a very curious manner. They drew upon the floor with chalk, a sufficient number of squares, chalking one all over, and leaving one open, alternately; and instead of black men and white, they had bits of stone and bits of wood. It was an admirable burlesque on gaming.

The chief satisfaction of these islanders when not engaged in war or in hunting, seemed to be that of lying at their ease in the open air, recounting tales of the bravery of their countrymen, and singing songs in honour of the Corsicans, and against the Genoese. Even in the night they will continue this pastime in the open air, unless rain forces them to retire into their houses.

The ambasciadore Inglese, The English ambassadour, as the good peasants and soldiers used to call me, became a great favourite among them. I got a Corsican dress made, in which I walked about with an air of true satisfaction. The General did me the honour to present me with his own pistols, made in the island, all of Corsican wood and iron, and of excellent workmanship. I had every other accoutrement. I even got one of the shells which had often sounded the alarm to liberty. I preserve them all with great care.

The Corsican peasants and soldiers were quite free and easy with me. Numbers of them used to come and see me of a morning, and just go out and in as they pleased. I did everything in my power to make them fond of the British, and bid them hope for an alliance with us. They asked me a thousand questions about my country, all which I chearfully answered as well as I could.

52

One day they would needs hear me play upon my German flute. To have told my honest natural visitants, Really gentlemen I play very ill, and put on such airs as we do in our genteel companies, would have been highly ridiculous. I therefore immediately complied with their request. I gave them one or two Italian airs, and then some of our beautiful old Scots tunes, Gilderoy, the Lass of Patie's Mill, Corn riggs are Bonny. The pathetick simplicity and pastoral gaiety of the Scots musick, will always please those who have the genuine feelings of nature. The Corsicans were charmed with the specimens I gave them, though I may now say that they were very indifferently performed.

My good friends insisted also to have an English song from me. I endeavoured to please them in this too, and was very lucky in that which occurred to me. I sung them 'Hearts of oak are our ships, ' Hearts of oak are our men.' I translated it into Italian for them, and never did I see men so delighted with a song as the Corsicans were with the Hearts of oak. 'Cuore di quercia, cried they, ' bravo Inglese.' It was quite a joyous riot. I fancied myself to be a recruiting sea officer. I fancied all my chorus of Corsicans aboard the British fleet.

Paoli talked very highly on preserving the in-

53

dependency of Corsica. 'We may, said he, have foreign powers for our friends; but they must be Amici fuori di casa, Friends at arm's length. We may make an alliance, but we will not submit ourselves to the dominion of the greatest nation in Europe. This people who have done so much for liberty, would be hewn in pieces man by man, rather than allow Corsica to be sunk into the territories of another country. Some years ago, when a false rumour was spread that I had a design to yield up Corsica to the Emperour, a Corsican came to me, and addressed me in great agitation: "What! shall the blood of so many heroes, who "have sacrificed their lives for the freedom of "Corsica, serve only to tinge the purple of a "foreign prince!"

I mentioned to him the scheme of an alliance between Great Britain and Corsica. Paoli with politeness and dignity waved the subject, by saying, 'The less assistance we have from allies, the greater our glory.' He seemed hurt by our treatment of his country. He mentioned the severe proclamation at the last peace, in which the brave islanders were called the Rebels of Corsica. He said with a conscious pride and proper feeling, 'Rebels! I did not expect that from Great Britain.'

He however shewed his great respect for the

British nation, and I could see he wished much to be in friendship with us. When I asked him what I could possibly do in return for all his goodness to me, he replied, 'Solamente disingannate il suo corte, Only undeceive your court. Tell them what you have seen here. They will be curious to ask you. A man come from Corsica will be like a man come from the Antipodes.'

I expressed such hopes as a man of sensibility would in my situation naturally form. He saw at least one Briton devoted to his cause. I threw out many flattering ideas of future political events, imaged the British and the Corsicans strictly united both in commerce and in war, and described the blunt kindness and admiration with which the hearty, generous common people of England would treat the brave Corsicans.

I insensibly got the better of his reserve upon this head. My flow of gay ideas relaxed his severity, and brightened up his humour. 'Do you remember, said he, the little people in Asia who were in danger of being oppressed by the great king of Assyria, till they addressed themselves to the Romans: and the Romans, with the noble spirit of a great and free nation, stood forth, and would not suffer the great king to destroy the little people, but made an alliance with them?'

He made no observations upon this beautiful piece of history. It was easy to see his allusion to his own nation and ours.

When the General related this piece of history to me, I was negligent enough not to ask him what little people he meant. As the story made a strong impression upon me, upon my return to Britain I searched a variety of books to try if I could find it, but in vain. I therefore took the liberty in one of my letters to Paoli, to beg he would let me know it. He told me the little people was the Jews, that the story was related by several ancient authours, but that I would find it told with most precision and energy in the eighth chapter of the first book of the Maccabees.

The first book of the Maccabees, though not received into the Protestant canon, is allowed by all the learned to be an authentick history. I have read Paoli's favourite story with much satisfaction, and, as in several circumstances, it very well applies to Great Britain and Corsica, is told with great eloquence, and furnishes a fine model for an alliance, I shall make no apology for transcribing the most interesting verses.

'Now Judas had heard of the fame of the ' Romans, that they were mighty and valiant men, ' and such as would lovingly accept all that joined

' themselves unto them, and make a league of amity
' with all that came unto them.

'And that they were men of great valour. It was
' told him also of their wars and noble acts which
' they had done amongst the Galatians, and how
' they had conquered them, and brought them
' under tribute.

'And what they had done in the country of
' Spain, for the winning of the mines of the silver
' and gold which are there.

'And that by their policy and patience they had
' conquered all the place, though it were very far
' from them.

'It was told him besides, how they destroyed
' and brought under their dominion, all other
' kingdoms and isles that at any time resisted them.

'But with their friends, and such as relied upon
' them, they kept amity: and that they had con-
' quered kingdoms both far and near, insomuch
' as all that heard of their name were afraid of them:

'Also, that whom they would help to a kingdom,
' those reign; and whom again they would, they
' displace: finally, that they were greatly exalted:

'Moreover, how they had made for themselves
' a senate-house, wherein three hundred and twenty
' men sat in council dayly, consulting alway for the
' people, to the end that they might be well ordered.

'In consideration of these things Judas chose
' Eupolemus the son of John the son of Accos,
' and Jason the son of Eleazar, and sent them to
' Rome, to make a league of amity and confederacy
' with them.

'And to intreat them that they would take the
' yoke from them, for they saw that the kingdom
' of the Grecians did oppress Israel with servitude.

'They went therefore to Rome, which was a
' very great journey, and came into the senate,
' where they spake, and said,

'Judas Maccabeus, with his brethren, and the
' people of the Jews, have sent us unto you, to
' make a confederacy and peace with you, and that
' we might be registered your confederates and
' friends.

'So that matter pleased the Romans well.

'And this is the copy of the epistle which the
' senate wrote back again, in tables of brass, and
' sent to Jerusalem, that there they might have by
' them a memorial of peace and confederacy.

'Good success be to the Romans, and to the
' people of the Jews, by sea and by land for ever.
' The sword also, and enemy be far from them.

'If there come first any war upon the Romans,
' or any of their confederates, throughout all their
' dominions,

58

'The people of the Jews shall help them, as the
' time shall be appointed, with all their heart.

'Neither shall they give any thing unto them
' that make war upon them, or aid them with
' victuals, weapons, money or ships, as it hath
' seemed good unto the Romans, but they shall
' keep their covenant, without taking any thing
' therefore.

'In the same manner also, if war come first upon
' the nation of the Jews, the Romans shall help
' them with all their heart, according as the time
' shall be appointed them.

'Neither shall victuals be given to them that
' take part against them, or weapons, or money,
' or ships, as it hath seemed good to the Romans;
' but they shall keep their covenants, and that
' without deceit.

'According to these articles did the Romans
' make a covenant with the people of the Jews.

'Howbeit, if hereafter the one party or the other,
' shall think meet to add or diminish any thing
' they may do it at their pleasures, and whatsoever
' they shall add or take away, shall be ratified.

'And, as touching the evils that Demetrius doth
' to the Jews, we have written unto him, saying,
' Wherefore hast thou made thy yoke heavy upon
' our friends and confederates, the Jews?

'If therefore they complain any more against
' thee, we will do them justice, and fight with thee
' by sea and by land.'

I will venture to ask whether the Romans appear, in any one instance of their history, more
truly great than they do here.

Paoli said, 'If a man would preserve the generous
glow of patriotism, he must not reason too much.
Mareschal Saxe reasoned; and carried the arms of
France into the heart of Germany, his own country.
I act from sentiment, not from reasonings.'

'Virtuous sentiments and habits, said he, are
beyond philosophical reasonings, which are not so
strong, and are continually varying. If all the professours in Europe were formed into one society,
it would no doubt be a society very respectable,
and we should there be entertained with the best
moral lessons. Yet I believe I should find more
real virtue in a society of good peasants in some
little village in the heart of your island. It might
be said of these two societies, as was said of De-
mosthenes and Themistocles, 'Illius dicta, hujus
facta magis valebant, The one was powerful in
words, but the other in deeds.'

This kind of conversation led me to tell him
how much I had suffered from anxious speculations.
With a mind naturally inclined to melancholy, and

a keen desire of enquiry, I had intensely applied myself to metaphysical researches, and reasoned beyond my depth, on such subjects as it is not given to man to know. I told him I had rendered my mind a camera obscura, that in the very heat of youth I felt the 'non est tanti,' the 'omnia vanitas' of one who has exhausted all the sweets of his being, and is weary with dull repetition. I told him that I had almost become for ever incapable of taking a part in active life.

'All this, said Paoli, is melancholy. I have also studied metaphysicks. I know the arguments for fate and free-will, for the materiality and immateriality of the soul, and even the subtile arguments for and against the existence of matter. Ma lasciamo queste dispute ai oziosi, But let us leave these disputes to the idle. Io tengo sempre fermo un gran pensiero, I hold always firm one great object. I never feel a moment of despondency.'

The contemplation of such a character really existing, was of more service to me than all I had been able to draw from books, from conversation, or from the exertions of my own mind. I had often enough formed the idea of a man continually such, as I could conceive in my best moments. But this idea appeared like the ideas we are taught in the schools to form of things which may exist, but do not; of seas of milk, and ships of amber. But I saw my highest idea realized in Paoli. It was impossible for me, speculate as I pleased, to have a little opinion of human nature in him.

One morning I remember, I came in upon him without ceremony, while he was dressing. I was glad to have an opportunity of seeing him in those teasing moments, when according to the Duke de Rochefoucault, no man is a hero to his valet de chambre. That lively nobleman who has a malicious pleasure in endeavouring to divest human nature of its dignity, by exhibiting partial views, and ex-aggerating faults, would have owned that Paoli was every moment of his life a hero.

Paoli told me that from his earliest years, he had in view the important station which he now holds; so that his sentiments must ever have been great. I asked him how one of such elevated thoughts could submit with any degree of patience, to the unmeaning ceremonies and poor discourse of genteel society, which he certainly was obliged to do while an officer at Naples. 'O, said he, I managed it very easily. Ero connosciuto per una testa singolare, I was known to be a singular man. I talked and joked, and was merry; but I never sat down to play; I went and came as I pleased. The mirth I like is what is easy and unaffected. Je ne

62

puis souffrir long temps les diseurs de bons mots,
I cannot endure long the sayers of good things.'

How much superiour is this great man's idea of
agreeable conversation to that of professed wits,
who are continually straining for smart remarks,
and lively repartees. They put themselves to much
pain in order to please; and yet please less than
if they would just appear as they naturally feel
themselves. A company of professed wits has
always appeared to me, like a company of artificers
employed in some very nice and difficult work,
which they are under a necessity of performing.

Though calm and fully master of himself, Paoli
is animated with an extraordinary degree of vivacity. Except when indisposed or greatly fatigued,
he never sits down but at meals. He is perpetually
in motion, walking briskly backwards and forwards.
Mr. Samuel Johnson, whose comprehensive and
vigourous understanding, has by long observation,
attained to a perfect knowledge of human nature,
when treating of biography, has this reflection:
'There are many invisible circumstances which,
' whether we read as inquiries after natural or
' moral knowledge; whether we intend to enlarge
' our science, or encrease our virtue, are more
' important than publick occurrences. Thus Sallust,
' the great master of nature, has not forgotten in

' his account of Catiline, to remark, that "his walk
" was now quick, and again slow," as an indication
of a mind revolving something with violent com-
motion (*a*).' Ever mindful of the wisdom of the
Rambler, I have accustomed myself to mark the
small peculiarities of character. Paoli's being perpetually in motion, nay his being so agitated that,
as the same Sallust also says of Catiline, 'Neque
' vigiliis, neque quietibus sedari poterat, He could
' not be quieted either by watching or by repose,'
are indications of his being as active and inde-
fatigable as Catiline, but from a very different
cause: The conspiratour from schemes of ruin and
destruction to Rome; the patriot from schemes of
liberty and felicity to Corsica.

Paoli told me that the vivacity of his mind
was such, that he could not study above ten
minutes at a time. 'La testa mi rompa, My head
is like to break, said he. I can never write my
lively ideas with my own hand. In writing, they
escape from my mind. I call the Abbé Guelfucci,
Allons presto, pigliate li pensieri, Come quickly,
take my thoughts; and he writes them.'

Paoli has a memory like that of Themistocles;
for I was assured that he knows the names of almost
all the people in the island, their characters, and

(*a*) Rambler, No. 60.

their connections. His memory as a man of learning, is no less uncommon. He has the best part of the classicks by heart, and he has a happy talent in applying them with propriety, which is rarely to be found. This talent is not always to be reckoned pedantry. The instances in which Paoli is shewn to display it, are a proof to the contrary.

I have heard Paoli recount the revolutions of one of the ancient states, with an energy and a rapidity which shewed him to be master of the subject, to be perfectly acquainted with every spring and movement of the various events. I have heard him give what the French call 'Une catalogue raisonnée' of the most distinguished men in antiquity. His characters of them were concise, nervous, and just. I regret that the fire with which he spoke upon such occasions, so dazzled me, that I could not recollect his sayings so as to write them down when I retired from his presence.

He just lives in the times of antiquity. He said to me, 'A young man who would form his mind to glory, must not read modern memoirs; m Plutarcho, mà Tito Livio; but Plutarch and Tit Livius.'

I have seen him fall into a sort of reverie, break out into sallies of the grandest and nol enthusiasm. I recollect two instances of this. 'V a thought? that thousands owe their happiness to you!' And throwing himself into an attitude, as if he saw the lofty mountain of fame before him: 'THERE is my object! (pointing to the summit), if I fall, I fall at least THERE (pointing a good way up), magnis tamen excidit ausis.'

I ventured to reason like a libertine, that I might be confirmed in virtuous principles by so illustrious a Preceptour. I made light of moral feelings. I argued that conscience was vague and uncertain; that there was hardly any vice but what men might be found who have been guilty of it without re-morse. 'But, said he, there is no man who has not a horrour at some vice. Different vices and different virtues have the strongest impression, on different men; Ma il virtù in astratto è il nutri-mento dei nostri cuori, But virtue in the abstract, is the food of our hearts.'

Talking of Providence, he said to me with that earnestness with which a man speaks who is anxious to be believed: 'I tell you on the word of an honest man, it is impossible for me not to be persuaded that GOD interposes to give freedom to Corsica. A people oppressed like the Corsicans, are cer-tainly worthy of divine assistance. When we were in the most desperate circumstances, I never lost courage, trusting as I did in Providence.' I ventured to object; But why has not Providence interposed sooner? He replied with a noble, serious and devout air, 'Because his ways are unsearchable. I adore him for what he hath done. I revere him in what he hath not done.'

I gave Paoli the character of my revered friend Mr. Samuel Johnson. I have often regreted that illustrious men, such as humanity produces a few times in the revolution of many ages, should not see each other; and when such arise in the same age, though at the distance of half the globe, I have been astonished how they could forbear to meet.

'As steel sharpneth steel, so doth a man the countenance of his friend,' says the wise monarch. What an idea may we not form of an interview between such a scholar and philosopher as Mr. Johnson, and such a legislatour and general as Paoli!

I repeated to Paoli several of Mr. Johnson's sayings, so remarkable for strong sense and original humour. I now recollect these two.

When I told Mr. Johnson that a certain authour affected in conversation to maintain, that there was no distinction between virtue and vice, he said, ' Why, Sir, if the fellow does not think as he ' speaks, he is lying; and I see not what honour ' he can propose to himself from having the cha-

F 2                                                    67

' racter of a lyar. But if he does really think that
' there is no distinction between virtue and vice,
' why, Sir, when he leaves our houses let us count
' our spoons.'

Of modern infidels and innovatours, he said,
' Sir, these are all vain men, and will gratify them-
' selves at any expence. Truth will not afford
' sufficient food to their vanity; so they have be-
' taken themselves to errour. Truth, Sir, is a cow
' which will yield such people no more milk; and
' so they are gone to milk the bull.'

I felt an elation of mind to see Paoli delighted
with the sayings of Mr. Johnson, and to hear him
translate them with Italian energy to the Corsican
heroes.

I repeated Mr. Johnson's sayings as nearly as I
could, in his own peculiar forcible language, for
which, prejudiced or little criticks have taken upon
them to find fault with him. He is above making
any answer to them; but I have found a sufficient
answer in a general remark in one of his excellent
papers: 'Difference of thoughts will produce
difference of language. He that thinks with more
extent than another, will want words of larger
meaning.' (a)

I hope to be pardoned for this digression,

(a) Idler, No. 70.

wherein I pay a just tribute of veneration and gratitude to one from whose writings and conversation I have received instructions of which I experience the value in every scene of my life.

During Paoli's administration, there have been few laws made in Corsica. He mentioned one which he has found very efficacious in curbing that vindictive spirit of the Corsicans, of which I have said a good deal in a former part of this work. There was among the Corsicans a most dreadful species of revenge, called 'Vendetta trasversa, Collateral revenge,' which Petrus Cyrnaeus candidly acknowledges. It was this: If a man had received an injury, and could not find a proper opportunity to be revenged on his enemy personally, he revenged himself on one of his enemy's relations. So barbarous a practice, was the source of innumerable assassinations. Paoli knowing that the point of honour was every thing to the Corsicans, opposed it to the progress of the blackest of crimes, fortified by long habits. He made a law, by which it was provided, that this collateral revenge should not only be punished with death, as ordinary murther, but the memory of the offender should be disgraced for ever by a pillar of infamy. He also had it enacted that the same statute should extend to the violatours of an oath of reconciliation, once made.

By thus combating a vice so destructive, he has, by a kind of shock of opposite passions, reduced the fiery Corsicans to a state of mildness, and he assured me that they were now all fully sensible of the equity of that law.

While I was at Sollacarò, information was received, that the poor wretch who strangled the woman at the instigation of his mistress, had consented to accept of his life, upon condition of becoming hangman. This made a great noise among the Corsicans, who were enraged at the creature, and said their nation was now disgraced. Paoli did not think so. He said to me, 'I am glad of this. It will be of service. It will contribute to form us to a just subordination. We have as yet too great an equality among us. As we must have Corsican taylours and Corsican shoemakers, we must also have a Corsican hangman.'

I could not help being of a different opinion. The occupations of a taylour and a shoemaker though mean, are not odious. When I afterwards met M. Rousseau in England, and made him a report of my Corsican expedition, he agreed with me in thinking that it would be something noble for the brave islanders, to be able to say that there was not a Corsican but who would rather suffer death, than become a hangman; and he also agreed with me, that it might have a good effect to have always a Genoese for the hangman of Corsica.

I must however do the Genoese the justice to observe, that Paoli told me, that even one of them had suffered death in Corsica, rather than consent to become hangman. When I, from a keenness natural enough in a Briton born with an abhorrence at tyranny, talked with violence against the Genoese, Paoli said with a moderation and candour which ought to do him honour even with the republick, 'It is true the Genoese are our enemies; but let us not forget, that they are the descendants of those worthies, who carried their arms beyond the Hellespont.'

There is one circumstance in Paoli's character which I present to my readers with caution, knowing how much it may be ridiculed, in an age when mankind are so fond of incredulity, that they seem to pique themselves in contracting their circle of belief as much as possible. But I consider this infidel rage as but a temporary mode of the human understanding, and am well persuaded that e'er long we shall return to a more calm philosophy.

I own I cannot help thinking that though we may boast some improvements in science, and in short, superiour degrees of knowledge in things where our faculties can fully reach, yet we should

71

not assume to ourselves sounder judgements than those of our fathers; I will therefore venture to relate that Paoli has at times extraordinary impressions of distant and future events.

The way in which I discovered it, was this. Being very desirous of studying so exalted a character, I so far presumed upon his goodness to me, as to take the liberty of asking him a thousand questions with regard to the most minute and private circumstances of his life. Having asked him one day when some of his nobles were present, whether a mind, so active as his, was not employed even in sleep, and if he used to dream much. Signor Casa Bianca said with an air and tone which implied something of importance, "Sì, si sogna, Yes, he dreams." And upon my asking him to explain his meaning, he told me that the General had often seen in his dreams, what afterwards came to pass. Paoli confirmed this by several instances. Said he, 'I can give you no clear explanation of it. I only tell you facts. Sometimes I have been mistaken, but in general, these visions have proved true. I cannot say what may be the agency of invisible spirits. They certainly must know more than we do; and there is nothing absurd in supposing that GOD should permit them to communicate their knowledge to us.'

He went into a most curious and pleasing dis-
quisition, on a subject, which the late ingenious
Mr. Baxter has treated in a very philosophical
manner, in his Inquiry into the Nature of the
Human Soul; a book which may be read with as
much delight, and surely with more advantage
than the works of those who endeavour to destroy
our belief. Belief is favourable to the human mind,
were it for nothing else but to furnish it entertainment. An infidel I should think, must frequently
suffer from ennui.

It was perhaps affectation in Socrates to say,
that all he had learned to know was that he knew
nothing. But surely it is a mark of wisdom, to be
sensible of the limited extent of human knowledge,
to examine with reverence the ways of GOD, nor
presumptuously reject any opinion which has been
held by the judicious and the learned, because it
has been made a cloak for artifice, or had a variety
of fictions raised upon it, by credulity.

Old Feltham says, 'Every dream is not to be
' counted of; nor yet are all to be cast away with
' contempt. I would neither be a stoick, super-
' stitious in all; nor yet an epicure, considerate
' of none*.' And after observing how much the
ancients attended to the interpretation of dreams,

* Feltham's Resolves, Cent. I. Resol. 52.

he adds, 'Were it not for the power of the Gospel, 'in crying down the vains† of men, it would appear 'a wonder how a science so pleasing to humanity, 'should fall so quite to ruin‡.

The mysterious circumstance in Paoli's character which I have ventured to relate, is universally believed in Corsica. The inhabitants of that island like the Italians, express themselves much by signs. When I asked one of them, if there had been many instances of the General's foreseeing future events, he grasped a large bunch of his hair, and replied, 'Tante, Signore, So many, Sir.'

It may be said that the General has industriously propagated this opinion, in order that he might have more authority in civilizing a rude and ferocious people, as Lycurgus pretended to have the sanction of the oracle at Delphos, as Numa gave it out that he had frequent interviews with the nymph Egeria, or as Marius persuaded the Romans, that he received divine communications from a hind. But I cannot allow myself to suppose that Paoli ever required the aid of pious frauds.

Paoli though never familiar, has the most perfect ease of behaviour. This is a mark of a real great character. The distance and reserve which

† He means vanity.
‡ Feltham's Resolves, Cent. I. Resol. 52.

some of our modern nobility affect, is, because nobility is now little else than a name in comparison of what it was in ancient times. In ancient times, noblemen lived at their country seats, like princes, in hospitable grandeur. They were men of power, and every one of them could bring hundreds of followers into the field. They were then open and affable. Some of our modern nobility are so anxious to preserve an appearance of dignity which they are sensible cannot bear an examination, that they are afraid to let you come near them. Paoli is not so. Those about him come into his apartment at all hours, wake him, help him on with his clothes, are perfectly free from restraint; yet they know their distance, and awed by his real greatness, never lose their respect for him.

Though thus easy of access, particular care is taken against such attempts upon the life of the illustrious Chief, as he has good reason to apprehend from the Genoese, who have so often employed assassination merely in a political view, and who would gain so much by assassinating Paoli. A certain number of soldiers are continually on guard upon him; and as still closer guards, he has some faithful Corsican dogs. Of these five or six sleep, some in his chamber, and some at the

75

outside of the chamber-door. He treats them with
great kindness, and they are strongly attached to
him. They are extremely sagacious, and know all
his friends and attendants. Were any person to
approach the General during the darkness of the
night, they would instantly tear him in pieces.
Having dogs for his attendants, is another circumstance about Paoli similar to the heroes of antiquity. Homer represents Telemachus so attended:

δύω κύνες ἀργοὶ ἕποντο.

HOMER. Odyss. lib. ii l. 11.

Two dogs a faithful guard attend behind.

POPE.

But the description given of the family of Patro-
clus applies better to Paoli:

Ἐννέα τῷ γε ἄνακτι τραπεζῆες κύνες ἦσαν.

HOMER. Iliad. lib. xxiii. l. 173.

nine large dogs domestick at his board.

POPE.

Mr. Pope in his notes on the second book of
the Odyssey, is much pleased with dogs being
introduced, as it furnishes an agreeable instance
of ancient simplicity. He observes that Virgil
thought this circumstance worthy of his imitation,
in describing old Evander. So we read of Syphax
general of the Numidians, 'Syphax inter duos

76

canes stans, Scipionem appellavit\*, Syphax standing
between two dogs called to Scipio.'

Talking of courage, he made a very just distinction between constitutional courage and courage
from reflection. 'Sir Thomas More, said he, would
not probably have mounted a breach so well as a
sergeant who had never thought of death. But a
sergeant would not on a scaffold, have shewn the
calm resolution of Sir Thomas More.'

On this subject he told me a very remarkable
anecdote, which happened during the last war in
Italy. At the siege of Tortona, the commander of
the army which lay before the town, ordered Carew
an Irish officer in the service of Naples, to advance
with a detachment to a particular post. Having
given his orders, he whispered to Carew: 'Sir,
' I know you to be a gallant man. I have therefore
' put you upon this duty. I tell you in confidence,
' it is certain death for you all. I place you there
' to make the enemy spring a mine below you.'
Carew made a bow to the general, and led on his
men in silence to the dreadful post. He there
stood with an undaunted countenance, and having

---

\* I mention this on the authority of an excellent scholar,
and one of our best writers, Mr. Joseph Warton in his
notes on the Æneid; for I have not been able to find the
passage in Livy which he quotes.

called to one of the soldiers for a draught of wine, 'Here, said he, I drink to all those who bravely 'fall in battle.' Fortunately at that instant Tortona capitulated, and Carew escaped. But he had thus a full opportunity of displaying a rare instance of determined intrepidity. It is with pleasure that I record an anecdote so much to the honour of a gentleman of that nation, on which illiberal reflections are too often thrown, by those of whom it little deserves them. Whatever may be the rough jokes of wealthy insolence, or the envious sarcasms of needy jealousy, the Irish have ever been, and will continue to be, highly regarded upon the continent.

Paoli's personal authority among the Corsicans struck me much. I have seen a crowd of them with eagerness and impetuosity, endeavouring to approach him, as if they would have burst into his appartment by force. In vain did the guards attempt to restrain them; but when he called to them in a tone of firmness, 'Non c'è ora ricorso, No audience now,' they were hushed at once.

He one afternoon gave us an entertaining dissertation on the ancient art of war. He observed that the ancients allowed of little baggage, which they very properly called 'impedimenta;' whereas the moderns burthen themselves with it to such a

78

degree, that 50,000 of our present soldiers are allowed as much baggage as was formerly thought sufficient for all the armies of the Roman empire. He said it was good for soldiers to be heavy armed, as it renders them proportionably robust; and he remarked that when the Romans lightened their arms, the troops became enfeebled. He made a very curious observation with regard to the towers full of armed men, which we are told were borne on the backs of their elephants. He said it must be a mistake; for if the towers were broad, there would not be room for them on the backs of elephants; for he and a friend who was an able calculatour, had measured a very large elephant at Naples, and made a computation of the space necessary to hold the number of men said to be contained in those towers, and they found that the back of the broadest elephant would not be sufficient, after making the fullest allowance for what might be hung by ballance on either side of the animal. If again the towers were high, they would fall; for he did not think it at all probable, that the Romans had the art of tying on such monstrous machines at a time when they had not learnt the use even of girths to their saddles. He said he did not give too much credit to the figures on Trajan's pillar, many of which were undoubtedly false. He

79

said it was his opinion, that those towers were only drawn by the elephants; an opinion founded in probability, and free from the difficulties of that which has been commonly received.

Talking of various schemes of life, fit for a man of spirit and education; I mentioned to him that of being a foreign minister. He said he thought it a very agreeable employment for a man of parts and address, during some years of his life. 'In that situation, said he, a man will insensibly attain to a greater knowledge of men and manners, and a more perfect acquaintance with the politicks of Europe. He will be promoted according to the returns which he makes to his court. They must be accurate, distinct, without fire or ornament. He may subjoin his own opinion, but he must do it with great modesty. The ministry at home are proud.'

He said the greatest happiness was not in glory, but in goodness; and that Penn in his American colony, where he had established a people in quiet and contentment, was happier than Alexander the Great after destroying multitudes at the conquest of Thebes. He observed that the history of Alexander is obscure and dubious; for his captains who divided his kingdom, were too busy to record his life and actions, and would at any rate wish to render him odious to posterity.

Never was I so thoroughly sensible of my own defects as while I was in Corsica. I felt how small were my abilities, and how little I knew. Ambitious to be the companion of Paoli, and to understand a country and a people which roused me so much, I wished to be a Sir James MacDonald*.

The last day which I spent with Paoli, appeared of inestimable value. I thought him more than usually great and amiable, when I was upon the eve of parting from him. The night before my departure, a little incident happened which shewed him in a most agreeable light. When the servants were bringing in the desert after supper, one of them chanced to let fall a plate of walnuts. Instead of flying into a passion at what the man could not help, Paoli said with a smile, 'No matter;' and turning to me, 'It is a good sign for you, Sir, Tempus est spargere nuces, It is time to scatter walnuts. It is a matrimonial omen: You must go

* Sir James MacDonald baronet of the isle of Sky, who at the age of one and twenty, had the learning and abilities of a professour and a statesman, with the accomplishments of a man of the world. Eton and Oxford will ever remember him as one of their greatest ornaments. He was well known to the most distinguished in Europe, but was carried off from all their expectations. He died at Frescati, near Rome, in 1765. Had he lived a little longer, I believe I should have prevailed with him to visit Corsica.

home to your own country, and marry some fine woman whom you really like. I shall rejoice to hear of it.'

This was a pretty allusion to the Roman ceremony at weddings, of scattering walnuts. So Virgil's Damon says,

> Mopse novas incide faces: tibi ducitur uxor.
> Sparge marite nuces: tibi deserit Hesperus Oetam.
>
> VIRG. Eclog. viii. l. 30.

> Thy bride comes forth! begin the festal rites!
> The walnuts strew! prepare the nuptial lights!
> O envied husband, now thy bliss is nigh!
> Behold for thee bright Hesper mounts the sky!
>
> WARTON.

When I again asked Paoli if it was possible for me in any way to shew him my great respect and attachment, he replied, 'Ricordatevi che Io vi sia amico, e scrivetemi. Remember that I am your friend, and write to me.' I said I hoped that when he honoured me with a letter, he would write not only as a commander, but as a philosopher and a man of letters. He took me by the hand, and said, 'As a friend.' I dare not transcribe from my private notes the feelings which I had at this interview. I should perhaps appear too enthusiastick. I took leave of Paoli with regret and agitation, not without some hopes of seeing him again. From having

known intimately so exalted a character, my sentiments of human nature were raised, while, by a
sort of contagion, I felt an honest ardour to dis-
tinguish myself, and be useful, as far as my situation and abilities would allow; and I was, for the
rest of my life, set free from a slavish timidity in
the presence of great men, for where shall I find
a man greater than Paoli?

When I set out from Sollacarò, I felt myself a
good deal indisposed. The old house of Colonna,
like the family of its master, was much decayed;
so that both wind and rain found their way into
my bed chamber. From this I contracted a severe
cold, which ended in a tertian ague. There was no
help for it. I might well submit to some incon-
veniences, where I had enjoyed so much happiness.

I was accompanied a part of the road by a great
swarthy priest, who had never been out of Corsica.
He was a very Hercules for strength and resolution. He and two other Corsicans took a castle,
garrisoned by no less than fifteen Genoese. Indeed
the Corsicans have such a contempt for their
enemies, that I have heard them say, 'Basterebbero
le donne contra i Genovesi, Our women would be
enough against the Genoese.' This priest was a
bluff, hearty, roaring fellow, troubled neither with
knowledge nor care. He was ever and anon shewing

me how stoutly his nag could caper. He always rode some paces before me, and sat in an attitude half turned round, with his hand clapped upon the crupper. Then he would burst out with comical songs about the devil and the Genoese, and I don't know what all. In short, notwithstanding my feverishness, he kept me laughing whether I would or no.

I was returning to Corte; but I varied my road a little from the way I had come, going more upon the low country, and nearer the western shore.

At Cauro I had a fine view of Ajaccio and its environs. My ague was some time of forming, so I had frequent intervals of ease, which I employed in observing whatever occurred. I was lodged at Cauro in the house of Signor Peraldi of Ajaccio, who received me with great politeness. I found here another provincial magistracy. Before supper, Signor Peraldi and a young Abbé of Ajaccio entertained me with some airs on the violin. After they had shewn me their taste in fine improved musick, they gave me some original Corsican airs, and at my desire, they brought up four of the guards of the magistracy, and made them shew me a Corsican dance. It was truly savage. They thumped with their heels, sprung upon their toes, brandished

their arms, wheeled and leaped with the most violent gesticulations. It gave me the idea of an
admirable war dance.

During this journey I had very bad weather.
I cannot forget the worthy rectour of Cuttoli,
whose house afforded me a hospitable retreat,
when wet to the skin, and quite overcome by the
severity of the storm, which my sickness made
me little able to resist. He was directly such a
venerable hermit as we read of in the old romances.
His figure and manner interested me at first sight.
I found he was a man well respected in the island,
and that the General did him the honour to corre-
spond with him. He gave me a simple collation of
eggs, chestnuts and wine, and was very liberal of
his ham and other more substantial victuals to my
servant. The honest Swiss was by this time very
well pleased to have his face turned towards the
continent. He was heartily tired of seeing foreign
parts, and meeting with scanty meals and hard
beds, in an island which he could not comprehend
the pleasure of visiting. He said to me, 'Si J'etois
encore une fois retourné à mon pais parmi ces
montagnes de Suisse dont monsieur fait tant des
plaisanteries, Je verrai qui m'engagera à les quitter.
If I were once more at home in my own country,
among those mountains of Switzerland, on which

you have had so many jokes, I will see who shall prevail with me to quit them.'

The General out of his great politeness, would not allow me to travel without a couple of chosen guards to attend me in case of any accidents. I made them my companions, to relieve the tediousness of my journey. One of them called Ambrosio, was a strange iron-coloured fearless creature. He had been much in war; careless of wounds, he was coolly intent on destroying the enemy. He told me, as a good anecdote, that having been so lucky as to get a view of two Genoese exactly in a line, he took his aim, and shot them both through the head at once. He talked of this, just as one would talk of shooting a couple of crows. I was sure I needed be under no apprehension; but I don't know how, I desired Ambrosio to march before me, that I might see him.

I was upon my guard how I treated him. But as sickness frets one's temper, I sometimes forgot myself, and called him 'bestia, blockhead;' and once when he was at a loss which way to go, at a wild woody part of the country, I fell into a passion, and called to him 'Mi maraviglio che un uomo si bravo può esser si stupido, I am amazed that so brave a man can be so stupid.' However by afterwards calling him friend, and speaking softly to him, I soon made him forget my ill humour, and we proceeded as before.

Paoli had also been so good as to make me a present of one of his dogs, a strong and fierce animal. But he was too old to take an attachment to me, and I lost him between Lyons and Paris. The General has promised me a young one, to be a guard at Auchinleck.

At Bogognano I came upon the same road I had formerly travelled from Corte, where I arrived safe after all my fatigues. My good fathers of the Franciscan convent, received me like an old acquaintance, and shewed a kind concern at my illness. I sent my respects to the Great Chancellor, who returned me a note, of which I insert a translation as a specimen of the hearty civility to be found among the highest in Corsica.

'Many congratulations to Mr. Boswell on his return from beyond the mountains, from his servant Massesi, who is at the same time very sorry for his indisposition, which he is persuaded has been occasioned by his severe journey. He however flatters himself, that when Mr. Boswell has reposed himself a little, he will recover his usual health. In the mean time he has taken the liberty to send him a couple of fowls, which he hopes, he will honour with his acceptance, as he will need some refreshment this evening. He wishes him a good night, as does his little servant Luiggi, who will attend him to-morrow, to discharge his duty.'

My ague distressed me so much, that I was confined to the convent for several days. I did not, however, find myself weary. I was visited by the Great Chancellor, and several others of the civil magistrates, and by Padre Mariani rectour of the university, a man of learning and abilities, as a proof of which he had been three years at Madrid in the character of secretary to the General of the Franciscans. I remember a very eloquent expression of his, on the state of his country. 'Corsica, said he, has for many years past, been bleeding at all her veins. They are now closed. But after being so severely exhausted, it will take some time before she can recover perfect strength.' I was also visited by Padre Leonardo, of whose animating discourse I have made mention in a former part of this book.

Indeed I should not have been at a loss though my very reverend fathers had been all my society. I was not in the least looked upon as a heretick. Difference of faith was forgotten in hospitality. I went about the convent as if I had been in my own house; and the fathers without any impropriety of mirth, were yet as chearful as I could desire.

I had two surgeons to attend me at Corte, a

Corsican and a Piedmontese; and I got a little Jesuit's bark from the spiceria or apothecary's shop, of the Capuchin convent. I did not however expect to be effectually cured, till I should get to Bastia. I found it was perfectly safe for me to go thither. There was a kind of truce between the Corsicans and the French. Paoli had held two different amicable conferences with M. de Marboeuf their commander in chief, and was so well with him, that he gave me a letter of recommendation to him.

On one of the days that my ague disturbed me least, I walked from the convent to Corte, purposely to write a letter to Mr. Samuel Johnson. I told my revered friend, that from a kind of superstition agreeable in a certain degree to him, as well as to myself, I had, during my travels, written to him from LOCA SOLENNIA, places in some measure sacred. That as I had written to him from the Tomb of Melancthon, sacred to learning and piety, I now wrote to him from the palace of Pascal Paoli, sacred to wisdom and liberty; knowing that however his political principles may have been represented, he had always a generous zeal for the common rights of humanity. I gave him a sketch of the great things I had seen in Corsica, and promised him a more ample relation.

Mr. Johnson was pleased with what I wrote here; for I received at Paris an answer from him which I keep as valuable charter. 'When you ' return, you will return to an unaltered, and I ' hope, unalterable friend. All that you have to ' fear from me, is the vexation of disappointing ' me. No man loves to frustrate expectations which ' have been formed in his favour, and the pleasure ' which I promise myself from your journals and ' remarks, is so great, that perhaps no degree of ' attention or discernment will be sufficient to ' afford it. Come home however and take your ' chance. I long to see you, and to hear you; and ' hope that we shall not be so long separated again. ' Come home, and expect such a welcome as is due ' to him whom a wise and noble curiosity has led ' where perhaps, no native of this country ever ' was before.'

I at length set out for Bastia. I went the first night to Rostino, hoping to have found there Signor Clemente de' Paoli. But unluckily he had gone upon a visit to his daughter; so that I had not an opportunity of seeing this extraordinary personage, of whom I have given so full an account, for a great part of which I am indebted to Mr. Burnaby.

Next day I reached Vescovato, where I was

received by Signor Buttafoco, colonel of the Royal Corsicans in the service of France, with whom I past some days.

As various discourses have been held in Europe, concerning an invitation given to M. Rousseau to come to Corsica; and as that affair was conducted by Signor Buttafoco, who shewed me the whole correspondence between him and M. Rousseau, I am enabled to give a distinct account of it.

M. Rousseau in his Political Treatise, entitled Du CONTRACT SOCIAL, has the following observation: 'Il est encore en Europe un pays capable de législation; c'est l'isle de Corse. La valeur et la constance avec laquelle ce brave peuple a su recouvrer et défendre sa liberté mériteroit bien que quelque homme sage lui apprit à la conserver. J'ai quelque pressentiment qu'un jour cette petite isle etonnera l'Europe (*a*). There is yet one country in Europe, capable of legislation; and that is the island of Corsica. The valour and the constancy with which that brave people hath recovered and defended its liberty, would well deserve that some wise man should teach them how to preserve it. I have some presentiment that one day that little island will astonish Europe.'

(*a*) Du Contract Social. liv. ii. chap. 10.

Signor Buttafoco, upon this, wrote to M. Rousseau, returning him thanks for the honour he had done to the Corsican nation, and strongly inviting him to come over, and be that wise man who should illuminate their minds.

I was allowed to take a copy of the wild philosopher's answer to this invitation; it is written with his usual eloquence.

'Il est superflu, Monsieur, de chercher à exciter
'mon zele pour l'entreprise que vous me proposez.
'Sa seule idée m'eleve l'ame et me transporte. Je
'croirois la reste de mes jours bien noblement,
'bien vertueusement et bien heureusement em-
'ployés. Je croirois meme avoir bien racheté
'l'inutilité des autres, si je pouvois rendre ce triste
'reste bon en quelque chose à vos braves com-
'patriotes; si je pouvois concourir par quelque
'conseil utile aux vûes de votre digne Chef et aux
'votres; de ce coté la donc soyez sur de moi. Ma
'vie et mon coeur sont à vous.'

'It is superfluous, Sir, to endeavour to excite
'my zeal for the undertaking which you propose
'to me. The very idea of it elevates my soul
'and transports me. I should esteem the rest of
'my days very nobly, very virtuously, and very
'happily employed. I should even think that I
'well redeemed the inutility of many of my days

' that are past, if I could render these sad remains
' of any advantage to your brave countrymen. If
' by any useful advice, I could concur in the views
' of your worthy Chief, and in yours. So far then
' you may be sure of me. My life and my heart are
' devoted to you.'

Such were the first effusions of Rousseau. Yet
before he concluded even this first letter, he made
a great many complaints of his adversities and
persecutions, and started a variety of difficulties
as to the proposed enterprise.

The correspondence was kept up for some time,
but the enthusiasm of the paradoxical philosopher
gradually subsiding, the scheme came to nothing.

As I have formerly observed, M. de Voltaire
thought proper to exercise his pleasantry upon
occasion of this proposal, in order to vex the grave
Rousseau, whom he never could bear. I remember
he used to talk of him with a satyrical smile, and
call him, 'Ce Garçon, That Lad;' I find this
among my notes of M. de Voltaire's conversations,
when I was with him at his Chateau de Ferney,
where he entertains with the elegance rather of a
real prince than of a poetical one.

To have Voltaire's assertion contradicted by a
letter under Paoli's own hand, was no doubt a
sufficient satisfaction to Rousseau.

From the account which I have attempted to give of the present constitution of Corsica, and of its illustrious Legislatour and General, it may well be conceived that the scheme of bringing M. Rousseau into that island, was magnified to an extravagant degree by the reports of the continent. It was said, that Rousseau was to be made no less than a Solon by the Corsicans, who were implicitely to receive from him a code of laws.

This was by no means the scheme. Paoli was too able a man to submit the legislation of his country to one who was an entire stranger to the people, the manners, and in short to every thing in the island. Nay I know well that Paoli pays more regard to what has been tried by the experience of ages, than to the most beautiful ideal systems. Besides, the Corsicans were not all at once to be moulded at will. They were to be gradually prepared, and by one law laying the foundation for another, a compleat fabrick of jurisprudence was to be formed.

Paoli's intention was to grant a generous asylum to Rousseau, to avail himself of the shining talents which appeared in his writings, by consulting with him, and catching the lights of his rich imagination, from many of which he might derive improvements to those plans which his own wisdom had laid down.

But what he had principally in view, was to employ the pen of Rousseau in recording the heroick actions of the brave islanders. It is to be regretted that this project did not take place. The father of the present colonel Buttafoco made large collections for many years back. These are carefully preserved, and when joined to those made by the Abbé Rostini, would furnish ample materials for a History of Corsica. This, adorned with the genius of Rousseau, would have been one of the noblest monuments of modern time.

Signor Buttafoco accompanied me to Bastia. It was comfortable to enter a good warm town after my fatigues. We went to the house of Signor Morelli, a counsellor at law here, with whom we supped. I was lodged for that night by a friend of Signor Buttafoco, in another part of the town.

Next morning I waited on M. de Marboeuf. Signor Buttafoco introduced me to him, and I presented him the letter of recommendation from Paoli. He gave me a most polite reception. The brilliancy of his levee pleased me; it was a scene so different from those which I had been for some time accustomed to see. It was like passing at once from a rude and early age, to a polished modern age; from the mountains of Corsica, to the banks of the Seine.

My ague was now become so violent, that it got the better of me altogether. I was obliged to ask the French general's permission to have a chair set for me in the circle. When M. de Marboeuf was informed of my being ill, he had the goodness to ask me to stay in his house till I should recover; 'I insist upon it, said he; I have a warm room for you. My servants will get you bouillons, and every thing proper for a sick man; and we have an excellent physician.' I mention all these circumstances to shew the goodness of M. de Marboeuf, to whom I shall ever consider myself as under great obligations. His invitation was given in so kind and cordial a manner, that I willingly accepted of it.

I found M. de Marboeuf a worthy open-hearted Frenchman. It is a common and a very just remark, that one of the most agreeable characters in the world is a Frenchman who has served long in the army, and has arrived at that age when the fire of youth is properly tempered. Such a character is gay without levity, and judicious without severity. Such a character was the Count de Marboeuf, of an ancient family in Brittany, where there is more plainness of character than among the other French. He had been Gentil-homme de la Chambre to the worthy King Stanislaus.

He took a charge of me as if he had been my near relation. He furnished me with books and everything he could think of to amuse me. While the physician ordered me to be kept very quiet, M. de Marboeuf would allow nobody to go near me, but payed me a friendly visit alone. As I grew better, he gradually encreased my society, bringing with him more and more of his officers; so that I had at last the honour of very large companies in my apartment. The officers were polite agreeable men: some of them had been prisoners in England, during the last war. One of them was a Chevalier de Saint Louis, of the name of Douglas, a descendant of the illustrious house of Douglas in Scotland, by a branch settled near to Lyons. This gentleman often came and sat with me. The idea of our being in some sort countrymen, was pleasing to us both.

I found here an English woman of Penrith in Cumberland. When the Highlanders marched through that country in the year 1745, she had married a soldier of the French picquets in the very midst of all the confusion and danger, and when she could hardly understand one word he said. Such freaks will love sometimes take.

Sic visum Veneri; cui placet impares
Formas atque animos sub juga ahenea
Saevo mittere cum joco.

HORAT. lib. I. Od. 33.

So Venus wills, whose power controuls
The fond affeçtions of our souls;
With sportive cruelty she binds
Unequal forms, unequal minds.

FRANCIS.

M. de la Chapelle was the physician who attended me. He had been several years physician
to the army at Minorca, and had now the same
office in Corsica. I called him the physician of the
isles. He was indeed an excellent one. That gayeté
de coeur which the French enjoy, runs through
all their professions. I remember the phrase of an
English common soldier, who told me, 'that at
the battle of Fontenoy, his captain received a shot
in the breast, and fell, said the soldier, with his
spontoon in his hand, as prettily killed as ever
I see'd a gentleman.' The soldier's phrase might
be used in talking of almost every thing which the
French do. I may say I was prettily cured by
M. de la Chapelle.

But I think myself bound to relate a circumstance which shews him and his nation in the
genteelest light. Though he attended me with the

98

greatest assiduity, yet, when I was going away, he would not accept of a single Louis d'or. 'No Sir, said he, I am nobly paid by my king. I am physician to his army here. If I can at the same time, be of service to the people of the country, or to any gentleman who may come among us, I am happy. But I must be excused from taking money.' M. Brion the surgeon major behaved in the same manner.

As soon as I had gathered a little strength, I walked about as well as I could; and saw what was to be seen at Bastia. Signor Morelli was remarkably obliging. He made me presents of books and antiques, and of every other curiosity relating to Corsica. I never saw a more generous man. Signor Caraffa, a Corsican officer in the service of France, with the order of St. Louis, was also very obliging. Having made a longer stay in Corsica than I intended, my finances were exhausted, and he let me have as much money as I pleased. M. Barlé, secretary to M. de Marboeuf, was also very obliging. In short, I know not how to express my thankfulness to all the good people whom I saw at Bastia.

The French seemed to agree very well with the Corsicans. Of old, those islanders were much indebted to the interposition of France, in their favour. But since the days of Sampiero, there have been many variances between them. A singular one happened in the reign of Lewis XIV. The Pope's Corsican guards in some fit of passion insulted the French ambassadour at Rome. The superb monarch resolved to revenge this outrage. But Pope Alexander VII. foreseeing the consequences, agreed to the conditions required by France; which were, that the Corsican guards should be obliged to depart the ecclesiastical state, that the nation should be declared incapable ever to serve the holy see, and, that opposite to their ancient guard-house, should be erected a pyramid inscribed with their disgrace (*a*).

Le Brun, whose royal genius could magnify and enrich every circumstance in honour of his sovereign, has given this story as a medaillon on one of the compartments of the great gallery at Versailles. France appears with a stately air, shewing to Rome the design of the pyramid; and Rome, though bearing a shield marked S.P.Q.R. receives the design with most submissive humility.

I wish that France had never done the Corsicans greater harm than depriving them of the honour of being the pope's guards. Boisseux and Maillebois cannot easily be forgotten; nor can the brave

(*a*) Corps Diplomatique anno 1664.

islanders be blamed for complaining that a powerful nation should interpose to retard their obtaining
entire possession of their country, and of undis-
turbed freedom.

M. de Marboeuf appeared to conduct himself
with the greatest prudence and moderation. He
told me that he wished to preserve peace in Corsica.
He had entered into a convention with Paoli,
mutually to give up such criminals as should fly
into each others territories. Formerly not one
criminal in a hundred was punished. There was
no communication between the Corsicans and the
Genoese; and if a criminal could but escape from
the one jurisdiction to the other, he was safe. This
was very easily done, so that crimes from impunity
were very frequent. By this equitable convention,
justice has been fully administered.

Perhaps indeed the residence of the French in
Corsica, has, upon the whole, been an advantage
to the patriots. There have been markets twice
a week at the frontiers of each garrison-town,
where the Corsican peasants have sold all sorts of
provisions, and brought in a good many French
crowns; which have been melted down into Corsican money. A cessation of arms for a few years
has been a breathing time to the nation, to prepare
itself for one great effort, which will probably end

in the total expulsion of the Genoese. A little leisure
has been given for attending to civil improvements,
towards which the example of the French has in
no small degree contributed. Many of the soldiers
were excellent handi-craftsmen, and could instruct
the natives in various arts.

M. de Marboeuf entertained himself by laying
out several elegant pieces of pleasure ground;
and such were the humane and amicable dispositions of this respectable officer, that he was at
pains to observe what things were most wanted
in Corsica, and then imported them from France,
in order to shew an example to the inhabitants.
He introduced in particular, the culture of pota-
toes, of which there were none in the island upon
his arrival. This root will be of considerable service
to the Corsicans, it will make a wholesome variety
in their food; and as there will thereby, of consequence, be less home consumption of chestnuts, they
will be able to export a greater quantity of them.

M. de Marboeuf made merry upon the reports
which had been circulated, that I was no less than
a minister from the British court. The Avignon
gazette brought us one day information, that the
English were going to establish Un Bureau de
Commerce in Corsica. 'O Sir, said he, the secret
is out. I see now the motive of your destination to

these parts. It is you who are to establish this Bureau de Commerce.'

Idle as these rumours were, it is a faſt that, when I was at Genoa, Signor Gherardi, one of their secretaries of state, very seriously told me, 'Monsieur, vous m'avez fait trembler quoique je ne vous ai jamais vu. Sir, you have made me tremble although I never saw you before.' And when I smiled and assured him that I was just a simple traveller, he shook his head; but said, he had very authentick information concerning me. He then told me with great gravity, 'That while I travelled in Corsica, I was drest in scarlet and gold; but when I payed my respeſts to the Supreme Council at Corte, I appeared in a full suit of black.' These important truths I fairly owned to him, and he seemed to exult over me.

I was more and more obliged to M. de Marboeuf. When I was allowed by my physician, to go to his Excellency's table, where we had always a large company, and everything in great magnificence, he was so careful of me, that he would not suffer me to eat any thing, or taste a glass of wine, more than was prescribed for me. He used to say, 'I am here both physician and commander in chief; so you must submit.' He very politely prest me to make some stay with him, saying, 'We have

taken care of you when sick, I think we have a
claim to you for a while, when in health.' His
kindness followed me after I left him. It procured
me an agreeable reception from M. Michel, the
French chargé d'affaires at Genoa; and was the
occasion of my being honoured with great civilities
at Paris, by M. l'Abbé de Marboeuf Conseiller
d'etat, brother of the Count, and possessing similar
virtues in private life.

I quitted Corsica with reluctance, when I
thought of the illustrious Paoli. I wrote to him
from Bastia, informing him of my illness, which
I said, was owing to his having made me a man
of so much consequence, that instead of putting
me into a snug little room, he had lodged me in
the magnificent old palace, where the wind and
rain entered.

His answer to my first letter is written with so
much spirit, that I begged his permission to publish it; which he granted in the genteelest manner,
saying, 'I do not remember the contents of the
' letter; but I have such a confidence in Mr. Bos-
' well, that I am sure, he would not publish it, if
' there was any thing in it improper for publick
' view; so he has my permission.' I am thus enabled to present my readers with an original letter
from Paoli.

## TO JAMES BOSWELL, Esq;

### OF AUCHINLECK, SCOTLAND.

STIMATISSIMO SIGNOR BOSWELL,

RICEVEI la lettera che mi favori da Bastia, e mi consolo assai colla notizia di essersi rimessa in perfetta salute. Buon per lei che cadde in mano di un valente medico! Quando altra volta il disgusto de' paesi colti, ed ameni lo prendesse, e lo portasse in questa infelice contrada, procurerò che sia alloggiata in camere più calde, e custodite di quelle della caso Colonna in Sollacarò; mà ella ancora dovrà contentarsi di non viaggiare quando la giornata, e la stagione vogliono che si resti in casa per attendere il tempo buono. Io resto ora impaziente per la lettera che ha promesso scrivermi da Genova, dove dubito assai che la delicatezza di quelle dame non le abbia fatto fare qualche giorno di quarantena, per ispurgarsi di ogni anche più leggiero influsso, che possa avere portato seco dell' aria di questo paese; e molto più, se le fosse venuto il capriccio di far vedere quell' abito di veluto Corso, e quel berrettone, di cui i Corsi vogliono l'origine dagli elmi antichi, ed i Genovesi lo dicono inventato da quelli, che, rubando alla strada,

non vogliano essere conosciuti: come se in tempo
del loro governo avessero mai avuta apprensione
di castigo i ladri pubblici? Son sicuro però, che
ella presso avrà il buon partito con quelle amabili, e
delicate persone, insinuando alle medesime, che
il cuore delle belle è fatto per la compassione, non
per il disprezzo, e per la tirannia; e cosi sarà rien-
trato facilmente nella lor grazia. Io ritornato in
Corte ebbi subito la notizia del secreto sbarco dell'
Abbatucci nelle spiaggie di Solenzara. Tutte le
apparenze fanno credere che il medesimo sia venuto con disegni opposti alla pubblica quiete; pure
si è constituito in castello, e protesta ravvedimento.
Nel venire per Bocognano si seppe, che un capitano
riformato Genovese cercava compagni per assassi-
narmi. Non potè rinvenirne e vedendosi scoperto
si pose alla macchia, dove è stato ucciso dalle
squadriglie che gli tenevano dietro i magistrati
delle provincie oltramontane. Queste insidie non
sembrano buoni preliminari del nostro accomoda-
mento colla republica di Genova. Io sto passando
il sindicato a questa provincia di Nebbio. Verso
il 10 dell' entrante anderò per l' istesso oggetto
in quella del Capocorso, ed il mese di Febrajo
facilmente mi tratterrò in Balagna. Ritornerò
poi in Corte alla primavera, per prepararmi all'
apertura della consulta generale. In ogni luogo

avrò presente la sua amicizia, e sarò deside-
roso de' continui suoi riscontri. Frattanto ella mi
creda

    Suo affettuosissimo amico

PATRIMONIO,
  23 Decembre, 1765.

             PASQUALE DE' PAOLI.


MUCH ESTEEMED Mr. BOSWELL,

I RECEIVED the letter which you wrote to me from
Bastia, and am much comforted by hearing that
you are restored to perfect health. It is lucky for
you that you fell into the hands of an able physician.
When you shall again be seized with a disgust at
improved and agreeable countries, and shall return
to this ill-fated land, I will take care to have you
lodged in warmer and better finished apartments
than those of the house of Colonna, at Sollacarò.
But you again should be satisfied not to travel when
the weather and the season require one to keep
within doors, and wait for a fair day. I expect with
impatience the letter which you promised to write
me from Genoa, where I much suspect that the
delicacy of the ladies will have obliged you to
perform some days of quarantine, for purifying

you from every the least infection, which you may
have carried with you from the air of this country:
and still more so, if you have taken the whim to
shew that suit of Corsican velvet* and that bonnet
of which the Corsicans will have the origin to be
from the ancient helmets, whereas the Genoese
say it was invented by those who rob on the high-
way, in order to disguise themselves; as if during
the Genoese government, public robbers needed
to fear punishment. I am sure however, that you
will have taken the proper method with these
amiable and delicate persons, insinuating to them,
that the hearts of beauties are formed for com-
passion, and not for disdain and tyranny: and so
you will have been easily restored to their good
graces. Immediately on my return to Corte, I
received information of the secret landing of Abba-
tucci†, on the coast of Solenzara. All appearances
make us believe, that he is come with designs
contrary to the publick quiet. He has however
surrendered himself a prisoner at the castle, and
protests his repentance. As I passed by Bocognano, I learnt that a disbanded Genoese officer was

* By Corsican velvet he means the coarse stuff made in
the island, which is all that the Corsicans have in stead of
the fine velvet of Genoa.

† Abbatucci, a Corsican of a very suspicious character.

seeking associates to assassinate me. He could not succeed, and finding that he was discovered, he betook himself to the woods; where he has been slain by the party detached by the magistrates of the provinces on the other side of the mountains, in order to intercept him. These ambuscades do not seem to be good preliminaries towards our accommodation with the republick of Genoa. I am now holding the syndicato in this province of Nebbio. About the 10th of next month, I shall go, for the same object, into the province of Capo Corso, and during the month of February, I shall probably fix my residence in Balagna. I shall return to Corte in the spring, to prepare myself for the opening of the General Consulta. Wherever I am, your friendship will be present to my mind, and I shall be desirous to continue a correspondence with you. Meanwhile believe me to be

Your most affectionate friend

PATRIMONIO,
23 December, 1765.

PASCAL PAOLI.

Can any thing be more condescending, and at the same time shew more the firmness of an heroick mind, than this letter? With what a gallant plea-santry does the Corsican Chief talk of his enemies! One would think that the Queens of Genoa should become rival Queens for Paoli. If they saw him, I am sure they would.

I take the liberty to repeat an observation made to me by that illustrious minister, whom Paoli calls the Pericles of Great Britain: 'It may be said of Paoli, as the Cardinal de Retz said of the great Montrose, "C'est un de ces hommes qu'on ne trouve plus que dans les Vies de Plutarque. He is one of those men who are no longer to be found but in the lives of Plutarch."

THE END.

For EU product safety concerns, contact us at Calle de José Abascal, 56–1°,
28003 Madrid, Spain or eugpsr@cambridge.org.

www.ingramcontent.com/pod-product-compliance
Ingram Content Group UK Ltd.
Pitfield, Milton Keynes, MK11 3LW, UK
UKHW012333130625
459647UK00009B/256